The Plimoth Colony Cook Book

A collection of "receipts" or "received rules of cookery" used in Plymouth from Pilgrim days to the end of the last century, together with a compendium of kitchen lore, quaint, curious, or quizzical.

The Plymouth Antiquarian Society

Collected by
Elizabeth St. John Bruce & Edith Stinson Jones

Compiled by
Rose Thornton Briggs & Dorothy Bitter Mayer

With illustrations by
Ellen Hatch Brewster

Edited by
Sally Larkin Erath

DOVER PUBLICATIONS, INC.
Mineola, New York

Copyright

Copyright © 2005 by The Plymouth Antiquarian Society

Bibliographical Note

This Dover edition, first published in 2005 by special arrangement with The Plymouth Antiquarian Society, is an unabridged republication of the ninth edition of *The Plimoth Colony Cook Book* first published by the society in 1957.

International Standard Book Number: 0-486-44371-X

Manufactured in the United States of America
Dover Publications, Inc., 31 East 2nd Street, Mineola, N.Y. 11501

The Plymouth Antiquarian Society

The Plymouth Antiquarian Society is the leading preservation organization in the town of Plymouth, Massachusetts, operating multiple historic sites, including the 1677 Harlow House, the 1749 Spooner House, the 1809 Hedge House, and an ancient Native American site, Sacrifice Rock. Since 1920, PAS has welcomed the public to explore the local past through tours, exhibits, and programs. The historic houses tell the story of everyday life in New England from the mid-1600s to the present, with period rooms featuring early American furnishings and domestic artifacts. The Society also offers a seasonal calendar of special events and a children's summer series on local history. Membership is open to the public.

The Antiquarian Society began as a grassroots effort to preserve local history by saving historic buildings from destruction. When the Town of Plymouth planned to demolish the 1809 Hedge House, concerned residents successfully organized to save the property by moving it to a nearby waterfront location. These far-sighted volunteers (originally all women) founded the Plymouth Antiquarian Society in 1919, and went on to preserve other historic properties and build a significant collection of American furnishings, decorative arts and textiles.

The 1677 Harlow Old Fort House is one of the few remaining seventeenth century buildings in Massachusetts' oldest town. The property is historically significant as the home of early Plymouth settler William Harlow, a farmer and town official, who also served as sergeant of the local militia and participated in King Philip's War. In 1676, Sgt. Harlow was granted permission to salvage material from the Pilgrim's fort-house on Burial Hill to use in the construction of his new dwelling. From the early nineteenth century, the Harlow House has been notable for the hand-hewn beams attributed to this source. Built as a sturdy family farmhouse hundreds of years ago, the Harlow House remains a welcoming place for children and families to enter and explore.

The 1749 Spooner House was home to one Plymouth family for over two hundred years, beginning with Deacon Ephraim Spooner, a successful local merchant and patriot during the American

Revolution. The Deacon's descendants, including mariners, farmers, abolitionists, reformers, and merchants, lived here into the 1950s, adding to and adapting the house to suit their needs. James Spooner, a lifelong bachelor and patron of music, was the last member of the family to occupy the house. In 1954, he bequeathed his home and generations of family possessions to be a historical museum. The two-story house, complete with its original furnishings, including china, paintings and New England furniture, offers a unique window into the American experience over two centuries.

The 1809 Hedge House is one of Plymouth's finest examples of Federal period architecture, featuring octagonal rooms in the main block, and a rare, intact carriage house. Built by sea captain William Hammatt, the house was altered by merchant Thomas Hedge, who purchased it in 1830 and added a three-story ell to accommodate his large family. The Hedges owned a Main Street store, a waterfront counting house, and "Hedges Wharf," a famous site because embedded in its surface was Plymouth Rock, thought to be the landing place of the Pilgrims. The Hedge family occupied the house until the death of the last resident, Lydia Hedge Lothrop, in 1918. Today, the Hedge House is a highly visible landmark on the Plymouth waterfront. Annual special events are held on the sweeping lawn overlooking scenic Plymouth harbor.

The Antiquarian Society's collection of Americana ranges from the late 17th to the mid 20th centuries. Society archives include Plymouth and area family papers, books, journals, and photographs. The Society holds an especially significant textile and clothing collection with an estimated 5,000 items.

For more information, please contact the Plymouth Antiquarian Society at P.O. Box 3773, Plymouth, MA 02361 or visit our website at **www.plymouthantiquarian.org**

To HELEN TABER BRIGGS

WE DEDICATE this book to the memory of Helen Taber Briggs, who as one of the founders of the Plymouth Antiquarian Society had the vision to perpetuate the Harlow Old Fort House as an example of an active Pilgrim home.

"She that is ignorant in cookery, may love and obey,
but she cannot cherish and keep her husband."

THE ENGLISH HUSWIFE
Gervase Markham (1615)

Harlow House 1677

COOKERY is a part of the program at the Harlow Old Fort House, built in 1677 by Sergeant William Harlow. The house is believed to be framed with timber from the original Pilgrim Fort, granted to Sergeant Harlow for his services in the Indian War. The Plymouth Antiquarian Society, which now owns the house, has made it a study of the home life and household routines of the Pilgrim century. There, hostesses spin, weave, dye yarn, make soap and candles, and cook in the great brick fireplace.

Pilgrim Breakfasts at the House

EACH summer a Pilgrim breakfast is served at Harlow Old Fort House, often called, simply, Harlow House. Tables are set in the house and under the trees in the gardens. Girls in Pilgrim costumes serve beans and fish cakes for this traditional meal.

HARLOW HOUSE MULLED CIDER

3 quarts cider
1½ teaspoons cinnamon
ginger, if liked

¾ teaspoon cloves
⅓ teaspoon nutmeg
⅛ teaspoon salt

Add the spices and salt to the heated cider and simmer 10 to 15 minutes. Makes 24 punch cup servings.

HARLOW HOUSE DOUGHNUTS
often called "Wonders"

1 cup sugar
2 eggs, beaten
1 cup milk
1 tablespoon butter, melted

flour
4 teaspoons baking powder
½ teaspoon nutmeg
½ teaspoon salt

Beat sugar, eggs, and milk together, add butter. Sift 3 cups flour with rest of ingredients, add to first mixture and stir until smooth. Add more flour, if necessary, to make a soft dough. Chill dough overnight. Roll out on floured board and cut with doughnut cutter. Fry in fat hot enough to brown a 1-inch cube of bread in 40 seconds (375 F.). As doughnuts rise to top, turn and brown on other side. Remove, drain on absorbent paper.

HARLOW HOUSE BAKED BEANS

2 pounds pea beans
1 onion
2 teaspoons mustard

½ cup molasses
½ teaspoon salt
⅜ pound salt pork

Pick over, wash, and soak the beans overnight. In the morning, drain, rinse, and cover with cold water, bring to a boil and cook until the beans can be pierced with a pin. Drain, put in bean pot with an onion in the bottom. Add mustard, molasses, and salt. Scrape and score the pork and bury it in the beans so that only the top shows. Cover with water and bake in a slow oven (300 F.) about 6 hours, adding water as needed. Uncover the pot for the last hour to brown the pork. 6-8 servings.

HARLOW HOUSE FISH CAKES

4 cups potatoes, cut in
1-inch cubes

1 cup salt fish, picked and
shredded

2 eggs, slightly beaten

Boil together potatoes and fish until potatoes are tender. Drain, mash, and beat in eggs. Drop by spoonfuls in hot fat, (390 F.) and fry for 1 minute. Drain on absorbent paper. 6-8 servings.

The natives of Jamaica, one of the earliest West Indian markets for New England fish, eat fish cakes almost identical with those of New England.

The First Thanksgiving

The brave little band of Pilgrims who landed at Plymouth Rock in 1620 almost perished in the long, hard winter because of inadequate supplies and no knowledge of how to conquer the wilderness in the New World. They found unexpected assistance in the last days of the winter when an armed Indian, Samoset, walked into their council meeting and amazed them by saying in English, "Welcome!"

Samoset, an **Abenaki** Indian, had heard of the landing of the English party. He helped them by acting as ambassador between the Pilgrims and Massasoit, the Wampanoag chief. Later two other English-speaking Indians appeared, Tisquantum, usually called Squanto, and Hobomok. Each in his way was a tower of strength in the early struggles of the Pilgrims. It is interesting to note that both names, Tisquantum and Hobomok, translated into English, mean "devil." They taught them the lore of the forest, methods of fishing and hunting, and first introduced them to the growing of corn which they planted along with their supplies of wheat and rye seed.

At the first harvest in the fall of 1621, Indians and Pilgrims joined for a harvest feast and celebration, with the Indian and Pilgrim hunters supplying deer, duck, and geese. Although the feast was in October, it was the forerunner of our own Thanksgiving celebration, first proclaimed by President Lincoln in 1863 for the last Thursday in November.

The First Harvest, 1621

"They begane now to gather in ye small harvest they had, and to fitte up their houses and dwellings against winter, being all well recovered in health and strength, and had all things in good plenty; for as some were thus imployed in affairs abroad, others were exersised in fishing, aboute codd & bass, & other fish, of which they tooke good stores, of which every family had their portion. All the somer ther was no wante. And now begane to come in store of fruits, as winter approached, of which this place did abound when they came first (but afterward decreased by degrees). And besids water foule, ther was great store of wild Turkies, of which they tooke many, besids venison, &c. Besids they had aboute a peck a meale a weeke to a person, or now since harvest, Indian corne to the proportion. Which made many afterwards write so largly of their plenty hear to their friends in England, which were not fained, but true reports.

Governor William Bradford,
Of Plimoth Plantation.
Boston (1856)

Of Early Plymouth Kitchens

A Well-Equipped Kitchen

A list for a "well-equipped kitchen" was gleaned from an inventory, taken in 1633, of the contents of the home of Will Wright, brother-in-law of Governor William Bradford. Master Wright's house stood in New Street, now North Street, in present-day Plymouth. The articles were in what the appraisers called the "first Roome," obviously the principal living room of the house. The other rooms were the "Buttery," the "Loft over the first Roome," the "Bedchamber" and the "Loft over the Bedchamber."

Item: 6 kettles, 3 yron potts, and a dripping pan
  7 pewter platters, 3 great ones and 4 little ones
  1 smale brasse mortar and pestle
  2 pint pots and 1 pewter candlestick
  1 pewter flagon, 2 pewter cups
  1 wine and 1 other beere bowl
  1 beaker and 1 caudle cup
  1 dram cup and a little bottle
  2 salt sellers
  3 porrengers
  ½ dozen old spoones, 3 pr. pot hookes
  1 old pr. of tongues and an old fire shovell
  1 pr. pot hangers
  2 smale old yron hookes
  1 pr. andyrons
  2 old yron candlesticks, and a pressing yron
  2 basons, 1 smale and another great one

The Brick Oven

The early brick oven had no flue. It was set in the back of the fireplace, and the fire was built in the oven itself. The smoke came out of the open mouth and went up the main chimney. When the oven was thoroughly heated the fire was removed, the food put in, and the oven door closed to retain the heat. The usual door was of heavy wood, cut to fit the mouth of the oven and furnished with a handle by which it could be set in place.

Later ovens were built with flues to carry off the smoke and so could be placed beside the fireplace, rather than inside it. An iron door was now hinged to the brickwork; sometimes an ash pit was provided to store ashes for making lye and soap.

How to Use a Brick Oven

Build a fire in the oven, using, first, kindling wood, then fairly dry wood. It will take about five logs. At the end of about two hours, when the top of the oven is white and glowing, rake out the embers, and put in the prepared food. At the back, put the beans which will stay overnight; the bread, pies, etc., in front. Close the oven door. When it is time to remove the food which needs the least cooking, do it as quickly as possible and close the door again immediately.

If you wish to use an old oven nowadays, especially one with flues, have a mason inspect it before use, as accumulated soot is a menace and fire hazard.

Peel

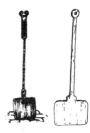

A peel is a long-handled shovel of iron, with a flat blade, used to take the embers and burning logs from the brick oven. The iron peel in the fireplace at the Harlow House is said to have been used by a lonely woman at the time of King Philip's War, to defend herself from a skulking Indian. In the encounter he was killed.

Wooden Peel

The wooden peel is like the iron one, but made of wood with a wider blade. Loaves of bread were carefully balanced on it and slid onto the oven floor.

Fireplace Equipment

A Lugstick was a stick of green wood, supported by "lugs" or projections part way up the chimney. From this hung the Pothooks by which the pots and kettles were suspended over the fire.

Great care was taken to renew the lugstick before it became charred. If it broke, it might spill the soup and scald the children sitting before the fire.

A Trammel was an over-size pothook, hung on the lugstick. It had an adjustable linked shank which could be hung at various levels on the notched edge, so the cooking pot could be hung higher or lower over the fire.

In the eighteenth century, the Swinging Crane superseded the lugstick as a support for pots. The Crane, hinged on one side of the chimney, swung to and fro like a gate. The housewife could swing her pot off the fire and season her soup without scorching her face, getting smoke in her eyes, or setting her apron on fire. It was a great convenience.

Cook Stoves

Cook stoves began to appear in the nineteenth century. One type made in a nearby town was advertised in the OLD COLONY MEMORIAL, Plymouth's weekly newspaper in 1822. This stove had three-inch round boiler holes, an oven, a large front door, and hearth. It was equipped with "one broiler, lid, and steam apparatus, fryer, tin tea-kettle, slide, circles, griddles, dripping pan, dipper, gravy dish, and one joined funnel." The cost was from twenty-four dollars to fifty dollars, according to size.

The maker claimed that such a stove would "wa... the room more equally, and with less than half the fuel than the common fireplace, while at the same time and without extra fuel, cooking and washing may be carried on for the largest families."

Cook stoves were accepted slowly. In 1844, Mrs. Leslie, in her HOUSE BOOK, is still urging upon her readers the merits of the cook stove, and pointing out the convenience of being able to stand upright while you cook!

Soups and Chowders

"Bean porridge hot, bean porridge cold,
Bean porridge in the pot, nine days old.
Some like it hot, and some like it cold;
Some like it in the pot, nine days old."
Old Nursery Rhyme

BEAN PORRIDGE

4 quarts liquor from boiled corned beef	2 cups white beans, soaked overnight and parboiled
½ cup cornmeal	2 cups hulled corn

Remove the fat from the beef liquor and strain. Sprinkle in the cornmeal slowly, stirring constantly, and add beans. (Cold baked beans may be used if desired). When the beans begin to soften, add hulled corn and boil another ½ hour.

Old-timers often froze the porridge, leaving a loop of string in it. It could then be hung up on a nail in the pantry or woodshed. This made it convenient for men working in the woods who could melt a chunk and boil again for their noontime meal. It was considered to be much better after nine days.

CLAM CHOWDER

1 quart soft-shelled clams	½ teaspoon salt
½ pound salt pork, diced	⅛ teaspoon pepper
1 medium onion, sliced	4 cups hot milk
3 medium potatoes, diced	2 tablespoons butter
common crackers	

Sand in chowder is an abomination, so wash clams carefully. Place in a kettle, add about 2 cups water, cover tightly, and steam about 20 minutes, or until shells open. Remove clams from broth, strain water through cheesecloth, let settle, and pour off top carefully, discarding sediment. Remove clams from shells, separate soft parts and reserve, after squeezing out black centers. Cut off black ends. Chop rest of clams coarsely.

Fry salt pork until light brown, reserve pork scraps. Fry onion in fat about 5 minutes. Put in kettle with pork scraps, chopped clams, clam liquor, potatoes, and seasoning. Add more water, if needed, to cover. Cook until potatoes are tender, add soft part of clams, and simmer 2 minutes more. Add hot milk and a few split common crackers. 6 servings. This chowder is much improved by standing at least an hour or longer before serving.

CLAM BROTH

Heat liquor from steamed clams, prepared as for clam chowder. Serve in cups as a first course. If desired, top each serving with a spoonful of unsweetened whipped cream.

Daniel Webster

Daniel Webster, statesman and orator, was one of the most brilliant political figures of the first half of the nineteenth century. As a rising young man, not yet widely known, he gave the oration at the two-hundredth anniversary of the landing of the Pilgrims. His eloquence caught the public imagination, established his reputation as an orator, and focused national attention on the Pilgrim story.

Webster was born in New Hampshire in 1782 and died at his estate in Marshfield, Massachusetts, one of the towns of old Plymouth Colony. He frequently fished in the Plymouth area and often drove over to go shooting with Mr. Hedge, whose home is now the Antiquarian House.

Once at the height of his fame, he went back to revisit the New Hampshire town where he was born. He rode up from the depot beside the stage driver. He did not give his name, nor did the driver show any curiosity.

"Wasn't there a family of Websters 'round here once?" the great man finally asked. "What became of them?"

"Fine family!" said the driver. "Fine family! They all turned out well except Daniel, but he went down to Massachusetts and got into politics, and I don't think he amounted to much!"

DANIEL WEBSTER'S FISH CHOWDER
one among many versions

"Four tablespoons of sliced onion were fried in the kettle, then the other things were added: a quart of well-mashed potatoes, a pound and a half of ship's biscuit (Boston crackers), well-broken, a teaspoon of thyme, half a bottle of mushroom ketchup, half a nutmeg, grated, a few whole cloves and some black pepper, a bottle of port or claret, a little mace, allspice, and some slices of lemon, six pounds of blue or white fish cut in slices and twenty-five oysters, with enough water to cover the whole an inch deep."

This was cooked slowly and stirred just enough to cook it evenly without burning.

PLYMOUTH FISH CHOWDER
a modern version

3½-4 pound cod or haddock	4 cups hot milk
1 2-inch cube salt pork	1 tablespoon salt
2 medium onions, sliced	½ teaspoon pepper
4 medium potatoes, sliced	common crackers

Cook cut-up fish in 2 cups cold water until fish falls away from the bones. Cut pork into tiny dice and fry until light brown. Remove pork scraps. Add onion to fat and cook slowly about 5 minutes. Pick fish from skin and bones. Add fish liquor and potatoes to fat and onions and enough water to cover potatoes. Boil until potatoes are almost tender, add fish and hot milk, seasonings, and pork scraps, if desired. Simmer 10 minutes. Pour chowder over halved crackers in tureen to serve. 8 servings.

OLD COLONY CLUB CLAM MUDDLE

1 quart shucked soft-shelled clams	2–3 tablespoons butter
2 cups water	2 tablespoons flour
Salt, cayenne pepper	6 cups milk

Grind hard parts of clams in coarse grinder, add soft parts, and heat to boiling in water. Season to taste, blend butter with flour and add, cooking gently and stirring constantly, until thickened. Scald milk (do not boil) and combine mixtures. Serve crackers separately.

OYSTER STEW

1 pint shucked oysters	¼ teaspoon pepper
2 tablespoons butter	½ teaspoon paprika
½ teaspoon salt	4 cups hot milk

Pick over oysters and remove any bits of shell. Cook gently in butter with salt, pepper, and paprika, until edges of oysters begin to curl and are plump. Add milk and serve at once. 4 servings.

Apparently there were no oysters in Plymouth in the Pilgrim days but Edward Winslow reports they could always get the Indians to bring them oysters from the warmer waters of Buzzards Bay.

LOBSTER SOUP
from an old manuscript notebook

Take the meat of half a lobster and chop very fine. (Lobsters are smaller now than they used to be, so take a whole one.) Put the "Tom" and liquid in a pot with three crackers, pounded fine, a piece of butter the size of an egg, pepper, salt, nutmeg. (The "tom" is the coral-colored roe and the green fat.) Add the chopped lobster and mix into a paste. Take a quart of milk and let it just come to a boil in a spider, then pour it over the paste and stir well. Then put over a slow fire and stir until it boils. See that it is well flavored. This will make enough for four persons.

LOBSTER SOUP
a modern version

1 medium lobster, cooked	2 tablespoons soft butter
3 common crackers	salt and pepper
	1 quart milk

Remove meat from lobster and chop fine. Mix with crackers, pounded fine, butter, and seasonings. Scald milk and add lobster mixture; heat, while stirring, until well-mixed. 4-5 servings.

FISH BISQUE

1 cup fresh fish, cooked and minced	1 tablespoon flour
4 cups liquor from cooked fish	1 tablespoon minced parsley
1 teaspoon salt	1 cup hot milk
½ teaspoon pepper	¾ cup dried bread crumbs
3 tablespoons butter	⅛ teaspoon soda
	cracker and lemon slices

Strain the liquor in which fish was boiled. Season 4 cups of this and simmer with fish 5 minutes. Blend butter and flour with parsley, add to fish, and cook slowly until slightly thickened. Combine milk, crumbs, and soda, add to fish mixture, stirring well. Simmer a few minutes and serve with crackers and lemon slices. 4-5 servings.

CORN CHOWDER

½ cup salt pork, chopped fine   2 cups canned corn
3 medium onions, diced   or corn cut from 6-8 ears
6 medium potatoes, diced   2 cups milk
2 cups boiling water   salt and pepper
common or pilot crackers

Fry salt pork until light brown. Remove pork scraps. Fry onion in fat about 5 minutes, add potatoes and water and cook until potatoes are almost tender. Add corn and milk and simmer about 5 minutes. Add salt and pepper as needed. Serve with crackers. 6-8 servings.

PEA SOUP WITH HERBS

2 cups green split peas   2 teaspoons salt
2 cups French sorrel leaves   2 teaspoons sugar
1 small carrot, diced   ½ tablespoon butter
1 small onion, diced   sprig of tarragon
2 branches celery   sprig of thyme
2 leeks   3 teaspoons fresh peas, cooked
2 raw potatoes, sliced   2 sprigs chervil, minced
1 ham bone   croutons

Soak peas overnight. In the morning, drain, put in pan with all other ingredients except fresh peas, chervil, and croutons. Add water to just cover and boil about 1½ hours, or until peas are well-cooked. Strain through sieve. Add fresh-cooked peas, chervil, and serve with croutons. 6-8 servings.

It is worthwhile to grow French sorrel just for this soup. If not available, substitute 1 teaspoon vinegar.

FRESH GREEN PEA SOUP
from an old manuscript notebook

Shell half a peck of fresh green peas, put the pods into a kettle. Cover with water and boil until tender. Strain out pods, add peas, and boil one-half hour. Reserve a pint of the peas and mash the rest into the soup. Add three pints of milk, the rest of the peas, and boil three minutes. Beat an egg, add a tablespoon each of butter and flour, mix gradually into the soup. Remove from fire, season with salt and pepper to taste. 6-8 servings.

POTATO SOUP

3 medium potatoes	½ teaspoon celery salt
1 small onion	dash cayenne
1 cup water	2 tablespoons butter
2 cups hot milk	2 tablespoons flour
2 teaspoons salt	crackers or croutons

Cut potatoes and onion very small, cook in water until potatoes are tender. Mash and add milk, seasonings, and rub through a sieve. Melt butter, add flour and then hot soup gradually. Cook about 5 minutes, being careful not to let it scorch. Serve with crackers or croutons. 4-5 servings. This soup is even better reheated the second day. Potatoes were not known in early Plymouth days; but after their introduction to New England, they became a staple crop.

TO MAKE AN ONION SOUP

from THE ART OF COOKERY MADE PLAIN AND EASY,
by H. Glasse, Edinburgh, Scotland (1791)

Take half a pound of butter, put it in a stew pan over the fire, let it all melt and boil it till it has done making any noise; then have ready ten to twelve middling onions, peeled and cut small; let them fry a quarter of an hour; then shake in a little flour and stir them around; shake your pan and let them do a few minutes longer; then pour in a quart or three pints of boiling water, stir them round.

Take a good piece of upper crust, the stalest bread you have, about as big as the top of a penny loaf cut small and throw it in.

Season with salt to your palate. Let it boil ten minutes, stirring it often, then take off the fire and have ready the yolks of two eggs beat fine with half a spoonful of vinegar; mix some of the soup with them, then stir it into your soup and mix it well and pour into your dish.

This is a delicious dish.

Mrs. Glasse was the author of the famous cook book which began its receipt for potted hare with, "First catch your hare."

Her book was still used in a Plymouth household twenty-five years ago. The book is now in the Plymouth Antiquarian House.

CUCUMBER SOUP

2 cups pared and diced cucumbers	½ cup soft butter
4 cups chicken stock	¼ cup flour
1 slice onion	salt and pepper
	2 cups hot milk

Cover cucumbers with water and parboil for 10 minutes. Drain. Add chicken stock and onion, and cook until soft. Rub through a sieve. Blend butter and flour, and add to soup, stirring constantly, while cooking, until slightly thickened. Season to taste and add hot milk. Strain and serve. 6-8 servings.

If desired, color green with a few drops of food coloring, and serve with salted whipped cream.

William Wood mentions cucumbers in NEW ENGLAND'S PROSPECT (1634), as does John Josselyn, in NEW ENGLAND'S RARITIES DISCOVERED (1672).

Fish, Shellfish and Clambakes

"Muskles and slammes (clammes) they have all the yeare long, which being the meanest of God's blessings, these people fat their hogs with. . . ."

John Pory (1622)

New England owes its very existence to fishing. The profits of off-shore fisheries in the New World spurred on the exploration of the New England coast and made English merchants willing to finance the establishment of permanent colonies here. It was this willingness that enabled the Pilgrims to raise money for their great adventure. Fish, supplemented by corn, kept the Pilgrims alive through the first hard years.

When the English merchants withdrew their support and sent no more ships to Plymouth, contact with England was maintained through the off-shore fishing fleet. Edward Winslow, Captain Myles Standish, John Allerton, and others, often sailed up to Maine in the colony shallop, and there arranged passage to England in a fishing vessel.

In the eighteenth and nineteenth centuries, fishing voyages to the Grand Banks, and the sale of cured salt codfish in the West Indies were important sources of income to Plymouth. Even today, Plymouth has an active fishing fleet. Its earliest maritime venture was a lasting one.

STEAMED CLAMS

Scrub clams thoroughly, put in a kettle with just enough water to cover the bottom and cover closely. Steam until the shells are well-opened (about 20 minutes).

Give each guest a soup plate full, an empty dinner plate for the shells, and a small bowl of melted butter with vinegar added to taste.

Open the shell, remove clam, dip in the butter sauce, and eat. The black end makes a natural handle.

PLYMOUTH CLAM PIE

1 quart shucked clams	salt and pepper
with liquor	pastry for two crusts
1 teaspoon butter	

Clean and pick over clams; chop hard parts, keeping soft parts whole but squeezing out black centers. Reserve about ¼ of the clam liquor.

Cover bottom of deep pie plate with pastry, add first the soft of the clams, then the hard parts. Dot with butter, add dash of salt and pepper, then the clam liquor. Cover with pastry, folding under the bottom crust to seal well. Prick top crust all over with fork. Bake 1 hour in a moderate oven (350 F.). 5-6 servings.

SCALLOPED OYSTERS

½ cup bread crumbs	1 pint shucked oysters
1 cup cracker crumbs	salt and pepper
¼ cup melted butter	4 tablespoons oyster liquor
2 cups milk or cream	

Mix bread and cracker crumbs and stir in melted butter. Put a thin layer of crumbs in bottom of a buttered shallow baking dish, cover with oysters, drained of their liquor and well cleaned, sprinkle with salt and pepper. Add half the oyster liquor and half the milk or cream; repeat and cover top with remaining crumbs. Bake in a hot oven (400 F.) about 25-30 minutes. 4 servings.

LITTLE PIGS IN BLANKETS

Season large oysters, removed from shell, with salt and pepper.
Wrap each in a slice of bacon, fasten with wooden toothpicks.
Fry in a large frying pan quickly, browning the bacon lightly.
Serve on toast. May be broiled, if desired.

CREAMED OYSTERS

4 tablespoons butter	2 cups milk
4 tablespoons flour	1 pint oysters, with liquor
½ teaspoon salt	1 cup diced celery, cooked
¼ teaspoon pepper	1 slice pimiento

Melt butter, stir in flour, salt and pepper; when well blended,
add milk. Stir over low heat until smooth and thick. Add oysters,
celery and minced pimiento. Cook gently about 3 minutes or until
the edges of the oysters curl. Serve at once on hot toast. 4 servings.

TO STEW CRABS

from THE WHOLE BODY OF COOKERY DISSECTED (1673)

Your crabs being boyled, take the meat out of the bodies or barrels and save the great claws and the small legs to garnish your dish. Strain the meat with some claret wine, grated bread, wine vinegar, nutmeg and a piece of butter. Stew them together a quarter of an hour on a soft fire in a pippen; on being stewed almost dry, put in some drawn butter, the yolk of an egg, a grated nutmeg, with the juice of oranges beaten thick, then dish the legs around them, put the meat into the shells and serve.

GREAT GRANDMOTHER'S RED FISH HASH

1 cup cold boiled potatoes	3 tablespoons butter
1 cup cold boiled beets	dash of pepper
1 cup salt codfish, freshened	1–2 tablespoons milk

Chop all together to form hash; brown in a spider or frying pan in the butter. Season with pepper and add only enough milk to moisten.

SALT FISH DINNER

Choose a thick piece of salt codfish weighing about ½ pound. Simmer in water for about 2 hours, changing water once.

Boil new potatoes, beets, onions, and, if desired, carrots.

Dice ⅛ pound salt pork, fry about 5 minutes or until pork is lightly browned. Serve in a bowl.

Each person flakes the fish, mashes the potatoes, cuts up the beets, onions, and carrots, adds a spoonful of pork scraps and fat, and covers with Drawn Butter Sauce.

DRAWN BUTTER SAUCE

4 tablespoons butter	salt
2 tablespoons flour	cayenne pepper
2 cups boiling water	1 tablespoon lemon juice

Melt butter, blend in flour, add boiling water, and cook, stirring constantly, until sauce is thickened. Season to taste with salt and pepper, add lemon juice. Makes about 2 cups.

BAKED FISH

Have the fish man clean a 3-pound haddock, making sure to remove the eyes. Place the rind cut from ¼ pound salt pork on the bottom of a baking dish.

Make a stuffing from:

12 common crackers, rolled fine	1 teaspoon salt
½ cup oatmeal	2 teaspoons Bell's poultry
1 egg	seasoning
hot water	

Mix all ingredients, wet with hot water to make quite moist.

Fill the fish and press the two sides together firmly. Lay flat in a baking pan over the pork rind, and add 2 to 3 cups hot water. Bake 2 hours in a moderate oven (350 F.), basting frequently. When nearly done, top with salt pork cut in 6 strips, and continue baking until fish is tender and pork lightly browned. Serve fish with the pork strips. 4-5 servings.

CREAMED FISH

1 pound cold boiled fish	1 tablespoon flour
1 tablespoon butter	1 cup milk or cream
salt and pepper	

Pick fish into small pieces. Melt butter in frying pan, add flour, and blend. Add milk or cream and cook, stirring constantly, until slightly thickened. Season. Add fish and when thoroughly heated, serve at once. 2-3 servings.

BAKED FISH IN SHERRY

1½ pounds haddock or flounder fillets	¼ cup sherry
powdered garlic	1 cup mushroom sauce OR
salt and pepper	1 can condensed mushroom
dried tarragon	soup
	buttered crumbs
grated cheese	

Lay fillets in a baking dish, sprinkle with seasonings and sherry. Add mushroom sauce or soup, top with crumbs and cheese, and bake in a moderate oven (350 F.) about 30-35 minutes, or until fish flakes easily when pierced with a fork. 4-5 servings.

"CAPE COD TURKEY" WITH EGG SAUCE

Remove head and tail from a 4 pound haddock or codfish; split and wipe with a damp cloth. Sprinkle inside with salt. Let stand overnight. In the morning rinse thoroughly, tie in cheesecloth and simmer gently in water about 30 minutes or until fish flakes easily when pierced with a fork. Place fish on a platter, surround with boiled potatoes and small boiled beets; also with fried salt pork scraps. Serve with sauce made by adding sliced hard-cooked eggs to Drawn Butter Sauce.

CUCUMBER SAUCE FOR FISH

1 large ripe cucumber	3 teaspoons vinegar
4 tablespoons salad oil	2 teaspoons salt
dash of pepper	

Pare and grate cucumber. Drain off excess water, add rest of ingredients. Heat gently over low heat. Good for all fish except salmon and mackerel.

CAPER SAUCE FOR FISH

1½ cups liquor from boiled mutton	2 tablespoons flour
	salt to taste
1½ cups milk	juice 1 lemon
1 tablespoon capers	

Strain liquor from mutton, add rest of ingredients, and heat slowly to boiling. Serve over baked or broiled fish.

The wholesomeness of the place and the healthfulness is accompanied with much plenty of fish everie day in the yeare, as I know no place in the world that can match it.   John Pory (1622)

INDIAN CLAMBAKE

Indian tribes used to spend their summers on Sandy Neck on Cape Cod, where fish, shellfish, and small game were plentiful. Today we can still find there heaps of shells and stones burned in their fires. Eight different kinds of shells have been found: soft and hard shelled clams, sea clams, quahogs, oysters, scallops, razor clams, and sea snails.

The bake was prepared by laying a stone nest on the sand and building a hot fire over it. The fire was kept burning for several hours, then the embers were raked aside, rockweed was spread over the hot stones; then the food, and another layer of rockweed on top.

Today we would cover the heap with canvas. Perhaps the Indians used green branches.

CLAMBAKE
modern style

The real beach clambake is still practical and lots of fun and good eating, but it does take time.

First, hollow out a pit in the sand, about a foot deep and large enough to hold the food for your party. Line the pit, bottom and sides, with rocks and build your fire in it. It should be a good hot fire and should burn for at least two or three hours to heat the rocks through. Next put a layer of rockweed on the hot stones. The menu is up to you. Clams, lobsters, chicken, corn, onions, potatoes, frankfurts, fish fillets, all are delicious. Tie each of the foods in a square of cheesecloth for easy removal. Cover the food in the pit with more rockweed and place a tarpaulin over all. Heap sand around the edges to keep the heat in. Let food steam for an hour or two, or until the clams open and the lobster is red.

BARREL BAKE

Use large galvanized barrels set on rocks so a fire can be built under them. Place rockweed and a little sea water in the bottom of the barrels, stack the food (prepared as for beach bake) that needs the longest cooking in the bottom. Top with more rockweed, add the barrel covers, and let steam about one hour.

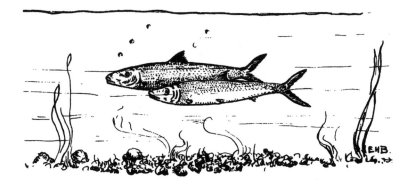

Meats, Poultry, and Game

Our harvest being gotten in, our governor sent four men on fowling, that so we might, after a special manner, rejoice together after we had gathered the fruit of our labors. They four in one day killed as much fowl as, with a little help beside, served the company almost a week. At which time, amongst other recreations, we exercised our arms, many of the Indians coming amongst us, and among the rest their greatest king Massasoyt, with some ninety men, whom for three days we entertained and feasted; and they went out and killed five deer, which they brought to the plantation, and bestowed on our governor, and upon the captain and others.

Edward Winslow
Plymouth (1621)

VENISON, as well as fish and wild fowl, is often mentioned among the foods the Pilgrims found at Plymouth; but Edward Winslow advised new settlers to bring beef with them and let the sailors salt it on shipboard.

In 1624 the first cattle were imported to Plymouth. More came in 1630, but for some years they were too valuable to use as food. When Will Wright died in 1633, his cow and calf were valued at £20, his house and garden at £10. Swine, goats, and sheep were also mentioned in the early inventories. As time went on, and cattle increased, their value went down. In 1649, a cow and a calf were worth only £5, 13 s., and 4 d.

In the early days of the colony, meat was usually boiled, broiled, or fried. Pots, gridirons, and frying pans are common, but only four spits are mentioned in the inventories filed before 1640. In the next ten years, twelve are listed, three being "jacks," that is, mechanical spits turned by clockwork. No doubt one of these was "the first jack brought to the Plymouth Colony," with which the Old Colony Club roasted their haunch of venison for the first Forefathers' Dinner in 1769.

A spit was a sharpened rod of iron thrust through the roast which was held in position by skewers passed through slots in the spit. The spit was then hung from lugs at the back of the andirons in the great open fireplaces and turned by a perspiring child who roasted nearly as fast as the meat.

Various devices were invented to mitigate this labor. The clock-work "jack" was one; the "tin kitchen" or "Yankee baker," was another. In the "tin kitchen" or "Yankee baker," the spit was enclosed in a bright tin reflector. This was so set that it needed attention only at ten or fifteen minute intervals. The principle has been revived in the modern reflector oven. If you wish to experiment with one of the old tin kitchens, line it with aluminum foil to reproduce its original reflecting brightness.

NEW ENGLAND BOILED DINNER

4 pounds lean corned beef	5–6 carrots, peeled and halved
1 medium cabbage, cut in eighths	2 pounds parsnips
2 pounds yellow turnip, peeled and sliced	2 pounds potatoes
	5–6 beets

salt and pepper

Simmer the beef in water for about 3 hours, then add prepared cabbage, turnips, and carrots. Let cook for ½ hour. Peel parsnips and potatoes and add, and continue cooking until vegetables are tender. Cook beets separately. Season to taste. Serve the meat on a large platter, surrounded by the vegetables. 5-6 servings.

RED FLANNEL HASH

Chop vegetables (except cabbage) left from a New England boiled dinner. Add a chopped raw onion. There should be enough beets to make a mixture a decided red in color. Add an equal amount of chopped corned beef and enough milk to moisten. Fry in bacon fat in a frying pan over low heat, until brown. Fold over like an omelet to serve. Fry any left-over cabbage separately in bacon fat and serve with the hash.

SPICED MEAT

2 pounds beef from round	1 teaspoon allspice
salt and pepper	¼ teaspoon garlic powder

Boil beef in small amount of water until tender. Cool, chop fine, add seasonings. Pour over the meat the liquor in which it was cooked, adding just enough to moisten. Mix well and pack solidly in a loaf tin. Chill well and slice to serve. 6-8 servings.

STUFFED FLANK STEAK

Spread dressing on a flank steak, roll up and tie to hold in place. Sear on all sides, in bacon or other fat. Place in a baking pan and pour over ½ cup tomato juice, or beef stock, if available. Cover and bake in a slow oven (325 F.) for 1½ to 2 hours or until tender.

FLANK STEAK DRESSING

3 slices stale bread	bacon fat
water or beef stock	½ teaspoon salt
1 small onion, minced	¼ teaspoon pepper
1 stalk celery, minced	¼ teaspoon mixed herbs

Crumble and moisten bread with water or stock. Cook onion and celery in bacon fat for a few minutes and add along with the seasonings.

POTTED BEEF

1½ pounds stewing beef	seasonings: salt, pepper,
1 medium onion, minced	powdered garlic, mixed herbs
2 tablespoons flour	2 cups stewed tomatoes

Cut beef in small pieces, place in a layer in a quart casserole. Sprinkle with onions, flour, and seasonings. Cover with tomatoes. Repeat layers until dish is full. Bake, covered, in a slow oven (300 F.) for about 2 hours. 5-6 servings.

The oldest directions say to cook this in a beanpot. An old pottery baking dish is good, and achieves a superb flavor.

FRIED PICKLED TRIPE

Parboil pickled honeycomb tripe about 3 minutes. Dry thoroughly and dip in beaten egg. Roll in flour and fry in a well-greased spider until brown on both sides.

BROILED TRIPE

Cut honeycomb tripe in pieces about 4 by 6 inches. Season with salt and pepper, sprinkle with flour, then dip in melted fat and sprinkle generously with sifted bread crumbs. Broil slowly 2 or 3 minutes on each side or until crumbs are brown. Serve with Mustard Sauce.

MUSTARD SAUCE

Fry 1 tablespoon minced onion in 3 tablespoons butter until onion is soft. Add 1 tablespoon vinegar and simmer 5 minutes. Moisten 2 teaspoons dry mustard with 1 tablespoon water and blend in, then add 1 cup brown gravy. Let simmer a few minutes and strain. Serve hot. Makes about 1¼ cups.

TOAD IN THE HOLE
a traditional English dish

1 pound beef steak	2 cups milk
1 egg	1 cup flour

salt and pepper

Cut meat in small pieces and place in a well-greased baking dish. Beat egg, add milk, beat in flour and seasonings. Pour over meat and bake 1 hour in a moderate oven (350 F.). Cooked meat may be used, if desired. 3-4 servings.

OLD NEW ENGLAND BEEFSTEAK PIE

1½ cups sliced onions	¼ teaspoon pepper
⅓ cup meat fat	3¼ cups boiling water
1½ pounds round steak cut in ½ inch pieces	1 tablespoon Worcestershire sauce
⅓ cup flour	1 cup raw potatoes, cut in ½ inch cubes
2 teaspoons salt	

pastry for topping

Fry onions slowly in hot fat until soft. Remove and save. Roll meat in mixture of flour and seasoning and brown in fat. Add boiling water and Worcestershire sauce. Sprinkle in any remaining flour. Cover, simmer until meat is tender (about 1 hour). Add potatoes, cook 10 minutes longer. Roll pastry into a rectangle ¼ inch thick. Mark portions with a knife. Pour meat into a well-greased oblong baking pan. Place onions on top. Cover with pastry. Bake in a hot oven (450 F.) for 30 minutes. 6-8 servings.

PASTRY FOR TOPPING

1 cup flour	⅓ cup shortening
½ teaspoon salt	1 egg

Sift flour and salt, cut in about ⅔ shortening; blend until fine as meal, as for pastry. Add egg. Roll out on floured board, dot with rest of shortening, fold and roll again.

BUBBLE AND SQUEAK
Fried Beef and Cabbage

When midst the frying pan in accents savage,
The beef so surly quarrels with the cabbage.

This is generally made with slices of cold boiled beef, salted and sprinkled with a little pepper, then lightly browned in a frying pan. The cabbage is cut up, boiled until tender, then squeezed dry and chopped fine. Remove beef from pan, add cabbage and heat through, stirring constantly. Lay the cabbage in the middle of a serving platter, and place the meat around it.

BOILED MUTTON WITH CAPER SAUCE
from DIRECTIONS FOR COOKERY IN ITS VARIOUS BRANCHES, by Miss Leslie, Philadelphia, Pa. (1850)

Wash and clean a leg of mutton, cut a small piece from the shank and strip the knuckle. Simmer in a kettle with water just to cover for 3 hours, skimming froth from the broth frequently. Remove from heat and let stand, covered, 10 to 15 minutes. Serve with a sauce of melted butter into which a cup of capers has been stirred. Mashed turnip and pickles are usually served with the mutton.

SMOTHERED FOWL AND OYSTERS
from an old manuscript notebook

Dress a good plump fowl as for roasting. Drain a pint of shucked oysters and fill the fowl. Sew it up and set in a kettle to steam with a rack under it to keep it out of the water. Add salt, pepper and some pieces of celery. Boil hard until fowl is tender but not broken. Serve with sauce made from the water in the kettle and one cup of cream thickened with flour. Add a pint of oysters and cook until they curl. Pour this over the fowl.

QUEEN'S MOUTHFULS

1 pound veal, poultry, or game, cooked or raw	1 teaspoon onion, minced
1 inch cube salt pork	2 teaspoons bread crumbs
salt and pepper	2 eggs
½ teaspoon nutmeg	2 tablespoons cream
2 sprigs parsley	¼ cup butter
	pastry

Mince meat, cook for a few minutes in salt pork fat. Add all other ingredients, except pastry, and cook over low heat for 5 minutes. Cool.

Roll out pastry to about the thickness of a silver dollar. Cut rounds 3 inches in diameter. Place a spoonful of the meat mixture on half the rounds, top with rest of pastry rounds, press edges together, and prick with a fork. Bake in a hot oven (400 F.) until pastry is lightly brown (about 10 minutes). Makes about 18-20.

VEAL POT PIE

½ pound salt pork	dough for dumplings
2 pounds veal from breast	1 cup cream
water	4 tablespoons flour
salt and pepper	2 tablespoons butter

Cut salt pork in ½ inch slices. Fry in a deep kettle until light brown. Add veal cut in cubes. Cook for ½ hour, turning often to brown on all sides. Add boiling water to cover the meat to a depth of about 1 inch, season to taste. Cook, covered, until meat is tender, about 45 minutes. Remove cover, add dumplings, taking each one up by tablespoons, cover and cook until dumplings are done (about 15 minutes). Remove dumplings and place around edge of serving platter. Put veal in center. Add cream to gravy in kettle, thicken with flour and butter rubbed together. Pour over veal and serve at once. 6 servings.

MOCK TERRAPIN

From FIFTY RECIPES, *collected by C. Hedges*
now in Antiquarian House, Plymouth

One pint of cooked, chopped chicken, one egg, boiled hard, one-half cup of stock, one-half cup of cream, livers, two tablespoons sherry, two tablespoons of melted butter, one tablespoon of lemon juice, nutmeg, cayenne, and salt to taste, one raw egg. After all is mixed, add the raw egg, lemon, and sherry.

PARSLEY SAUCE FOR MEAT

from an old manuscript notebook

Scald a large handful of parsley in boiling water that has some salt in it. When tender, chop it fine and stir into some rather thick melted butter. There should be sufficient parsley to make the sauce green and parsley should not be put to melted butter until about to be served otherwise it will be brown. The thick melted butter is made by rubbing flour into the butter and then melting over mild heat.

MINT SAUCE FOR LAMB

from an old manuscript notebook

Pick the mint leaves off the stalks, wash and dry them carefully. Chop them with a sharp knife quickly to preserve their green color. Put into a boat, add sufficient vinegar to make it liquid, and powdered sugar to take off the acidity of the vinegar.

The breakfast of the Pilgrim colonists generally comprised milk and hasty pudding or rye pudding and bread with pea or bean soup, and stew, flavored with pork; or salt fish.

For dinner, bean soup or baked beans and pork; stewed peas, squash, turnips, parsnips and onions. Fresh fish was common but mutton and beef were rarely seen. Butter and cheese, after the first few years were plenty, except among the very poor.

THE PILGRIM REPUBLIC
J. A. Goodwin (1888)

PICKLED LAMBS' TONGUES

12 fresh lambs' tongues	2 whole cloves
water to cover	2 whole allspice
1 cup water, additional	OR
3 cups vinegar	½ teaspoon each, powdered

Boil lambs' tongues in water to cover until tender. Cool in liquor, then skin and trim. Boil together the rest of the ingredients, cool and pour over tongues. Serve these split lengthwise. This is a delicious hot-weather dish. 5-6 servings.

Will Wright, Governor William Bradford's brother-in-law, died in 1633, leaving a ewe lamb to the church at Plymouth "to have and to hold the same forever."

PLYMOUTH SUCCOTASH

Traditionally, Succotash is served on Forefathers' Day, December 21, the anniversary of the landing of the Pilgrims at Plymouth. It was first celebrated in 1769, when the Old Colony Club met and dined together in "commemoration of the landing of their worthy ancestors in this place."

1 quart pea beans	5 quarts hulled corn
6 pounds corned beef	1 medium turnip
5 pounds fowl	5 medium potatoes (if desired)

Soak beans overnight, then cook and mash. This makes the thickening. Boil beef and fowl until tender, and save liquor; cut up turnip and potatoes and cook in the liquor. Cut the beef and fowl in 1½ inch cubes. Combine all the ingredients and let boil together for about 1 hour. Stir frequently to keep from sticking. Let cool, always uncovered. Stir occasionally to keep from souring. Serve in soup plates. This is better the second and third day. The Pilgrims used to freeze it, cutting off chunks at a time and reheating.

SALT PORK WITH MILK GRAVY

¾ pound lean salt pork	2 tablespoons flour
1 cup cold milk	

Cube salt pork and fry until crisp. Drain off excess fat, leaving 2 tablespoons in pan. Add flour and blend until smooth. Add milk and cook, stirring constantly, until thickened. Add pork cubes and serve over hot baked or mashed potatoes. 2-3 servings.

Wild Game

In this land they have plenty of game, deere, and turkies as large and fat as in any other place. . . .

From the beginning of September till the end of March, their bay in a manner is covered wtih all sorts of water fowl in such swarms and multitudes as is rather admirable than creditable.

John Pory (1622)

VENISON STEAK

from an old manuscript notebook

Broil steaks quickly over a hot fire. When sufficiently done, pour over 2 tablespoons currant jelly, melted with a piece of butter the size of a walnut. Season with salt and pepper and serve very hot.

TO BAKE RED DEER

from THE COMPLEAT COOK, London (1671)

Parboil it and sauce it in vinegar. Then lard it very thick, insert thin strips of salt pork through the meat and season with pepper, nutmeg, and ginger.

Put it in a deep Pye, with a good store of sweet butter and let it bake.

When it is baked, take a pint of Hippocras (red wine, spiced and sweetened), half a pound of sweet butter, two or three nutmegs, pour it into the Pye in the oven and let it lie and soak an hour.

Then take it out and when it is cold, close the vent hole.

ROAST VENISON

6 to 8 pound roast of venison	6 strips of bacon
flour, salt and pepper	1 large onion
2 cups tomato soup	

Wipe roast with a cloth soaked in vinegar. Dredge with flour that has been well salted and peppered. Lay strips of bacon over the top, add onion rings and fasten to roast with toothpicks. Roast in a very hot oven (500 F.) for about 15 minutes, then reduce the heat to moderate (350 F.) and roast 20 minutes to the pound. About 40 minutes before the end of cooking time, pour soup over roast. Continue cooking, basting occasionally. The soup makes a delicious gravy for the roast. 10-12 servings.

ROAST WILD DUCK

Canvasback, Mallard, Teal or any other varieties of wild fowl are prepared by first plucking, dressing and singeing to remove pin feathers; then the heads are removed and birds well wiped.

Do not, if it can be avoided, put in water. Next, season slightly with salt and pepper and place in a very hot oven (500 F.) to cook.

The flesh should be rare but not raw; 20 to 25 minutes in a hot oven will cook a medium-sized duck perfectly.

Use juices in pan for a sauce, season to suit taste.

All About Coot

The traditional rule for cooking coot, a duck with a strong fish flavor, is this:

Clean and truss your coot. Boil for 4 hours in a large kettle into which you have put a clean brick. Then throw out the coot and serve the brick! Coot is shot in the fall, from a dory off-shore; a cold stormy dawn is the best time.

TO PREPARE COOT

Pluck and clean the coot, as for roasting, at least a day or two before it is to be cooked. To take the strong fishy flavor away, fill the coot with earth and bury it for twenty-four hours. Dig it up, clean and wash thoroughly, and it can be roasted like a black duck.

This may sound drastic, but it is true!

FRIED COOT BREAST

Cut the breast off a coot, discarding the rest. Trim off all the yellow fat, soak for 3-4 hours in a mixture of ½ cup vinegar, 1 teaspoon baking soda, and water to cover. Drain, rinse, and drain again. Fry in hot bacon fat or butter; when done, add a glass of currant jelly. Some people add a little sherry wine. Serve with wild rice, or common rice, buttered.

Vegetables

If fresh meat is wanting to fill up our dish
We have carrots and turnips whenever we wish.
For pottage and puddings and custards and pies
Our pumpkins and parsnips are common supplies;
We have pumpkins at morning and pumpkins at noon,
If 'twere not for pumpkins we should be undoone.

GUIDE TO PLYMOUTH,
William S. Russell (1846)

Mr. Russell says of this poem: ". . . composed about 1630 and taken from the lips of an old lady at the advanced age of ninety-six!"

STEWED PUMPKINS
from NEW ENGLAND'S RARITIES DISCOVERED
John Josselyn (1672)

Slice them when ripe, and cut them in dice, and so fill a pot with them of two or 3 gallons. Stew them upon a gentle fire a whole day and as they sink then fill again with fresh pumpkins, not putting any liquor to them, and when it is stewed enough it will look like baked apples. Dish this, putting butter to it, a little vinegar, some spice, as ginger, which makes them taste like an apple; and store it up to be eaten with fish or flesh.

PARSNIP STEW

2 slices fat salt pork	½ teaspoon salt
1 large onion, diced	boiling water
4 large potatoes	dumplings
4 parsnips	1 cup cream, heated

Dice salt pork and fry until lightly browned. Add onion and cook until golden brown. Peel and cut in pieces the potatoes and parsnips, add to the pork and onions with salt in a large kettle. Cover with boiling water and cook until the vegetables are almost tender (about 20 minutes). Add dumplings to the top of the stew, cover and cook until the dumplings are light and tender (about 15 minutes). Remove dumplings to a hot platter, add the hot cream to the stew and pour over the dumplings. 4-5 servings.

DUMPLINGS

1 cup flour	1 tablespoon shortening
2 teaspoons baking powder	⅓ cup milk
½ teaspoon salt	

Sift dry ingredients, cut in shortening as for pastry, add milk. Dip a tablespoon into stew, then dip up a spoonful of batter at a time and drop on top of stew. Makes 4-5 dumplings.

LUNCHEON PARSNIPS

Cut peeled parsnips and potatoes into pieces about ½ inch thick. Parboil about 10 minutes in a small amount of water; drain and lay in a baking dish. Half cover the top with thin slices of salt pork. Bake in a moderate oven (350 F.) until pork is delicately browned and the vegetables are tender.

SCALLOPED TOMATOES

Scald and peel 6 large tomatoes. Place a layer in a buttered baking dish, season with a finely minced onion. Add salt and pepper to taste. Cover with a layer of bread or cracker crumbs. Repeat until dish is full, ending with a layer of crumbs. Dot with butter and bake in a moderate oven (350 F.) about 45 minutes. 3-4 servings.

A couple of generations ago, tomatoes were called "Love Apples" and grown in flower gardens. They were considered poisonous to eat.

COLE SLAW

¼ cup vinegar	¼ teaspoon pepper
1 tablespoon sugar	2 eggs
1 tablespoon butter	2 tablespoons cream
1½ teaspoons salt	3 cups shredded cabbage

Heat vinegar, sugar, butter, and seasonings to the boiling point. Beat the eggs, add a little of the hot mixture, while stirring, then return to the hot mixture and cook over hot water until it thickens. Stir in cream and pour over cabbage.

If you wish to eat clean dry cabbage cut up fine and sprinkle with salt and vinegar, there is nothing better for the health. That you may eat it with a better appetite, sprinkle it with honey and vinegar mixed together.

DE AGRICULTURA
Cato the Censor (234-149 B.C.)

COLLY FLOWERS WITH BUTTER

An old receipt goes like this:

When they are well picked, boil them over a quick fire, with water, salt and two or three cloves. When they are boiled, drain them dry, and lay them in plates or little dishes, pour over them a thick Sauce made with Butter, Vinegar, Salt, Nutmeg, White Pepper, and slices of Lemon. Knead your butter with a little Flower before you melt it, to thicken the Sauce.

A modern version would be this:

Cook cauliflower in boiling water until tender. Drain and serve with Butter Sauce:

1½ tablespoons butter	a few grains nutmeg
1 tablespoon flour	1 tablespoon vinegar
¼ teaspoon salt	1 slice lemon, diced
¼ teaspoon pepper	1 cup water

Cream together butter, flour, salt, and pepper, and nutmeg. Cook over hot water with vinegar until slightly thickened. Add lemon. Add water slowly and cook, stirring often, until well mixed. Pour over cauliflower. 3 servings.

PLYMOUTH CORN PUDDING

1 egg	½ teaspoon sugar
1 cup milk	½ tablespoon melted butter
½ teaspoon salt	few grains cayenne pepper
1 cup cooked corn, scraped from cob	

Beat the egg, add milk, seasonings, butter and corn. Turn into a buttered baking dish and bake in a moderate oven (350 F.) about 45 minutes or until center is firm like a custard. 4 servings.

"Five kernels of corn in a row,
One for the blackbird, one for the crow,
One for the cutworm and two to grow!"

A little pageant is held each spring at Harlow Old Fort House, called "The Corn Planting." The girls plant flax; the boys, directed by the Indian Squanto, plant the corn with three herrings in each hill. It has been found that in the hills so fertilized, the corn stalks grow two feet taller than in the hills without the fish.

The Pilgrims had their first sight of Indian corn at Cape Cod. While the Mayflower still lay at anchor in Provincetown Harbor, an exploring party, led by Captain Myles Standish, stumbled upon a cache of Indian corn, "some red, some yellow, and others mixed with blue." As was the Indian custom, it had been carefully stored in baskets, "as much as two of us could lift up from the ground," and buried under a mound of sand. The Pilgrims took what they could carry but could not find the Indian owners. After they were settled, however, they sought out the Indians and repaid them.

Corn was grown by the Indians who once inhabited Plymouth. Champlain's map of the harbor shows many cornfields dotting the shores. Between his visit to these shores and the coming of the Pilgrims, these Indians had perished in a devastating epidemic; but the sight of their cornfields was one of the reasons the Pilgrims chose Plymouth for their first settlement.

In the spring of 1621, their first in this country, soon after the Mayflower had left for England, the Pilgrims, "as many as were able," began to plant corn under the direction of the Indian Squanto. He, says Governor William Bradford, "taught them how to set it, and afterwards how to dress and tend it." He also taught them how to set herring with the corn as fertilizer, and showed them how to catch the herring in the brook beside the settlement. Indian corn became the staple food in Plymouth. It kept the colony alive in its early days and was so indispensable it was used for money. You could pay your debts with corn. Corn was used in place of the English wheat which fared badly in the first few seasons, and was used more often as a substitute for bread than as a vegetable. Hulled corn and succotash became staple dishes, both taught the Pilgrims by the Indians. (See the chapter on Breads, etc., for other corn receipts.)

HULLED CORN
This receipt is used by Harlow House in their "Class of
17th Century Cooking."

Tie a quart of oak ashes in a flannel bag, and put it with three gallons of cold water into an iron kettle. Let it boil and become lye; that is, until the water becomes black. Take out the bag, and put in four quarts of corn. The "smutty-white" corn is the proper kind to use. Boil until the hulls have all started to loosen, stirring well with a wooden spoon. (Wood and iron are the only substances safe to use with lye.)

Now put the kernels in a large pan of cold water, and rub thoroughly with the hand to remove the hulls. Change the water five or six times and wash and rub until the corn is clean and white. Keep in cold water overnight.

In the morning, drain, cover with fresh cold water, and simmer four hours or until soft and fluffy. Skim as necessary, and add fresh water several times during the simmering.

HULLED CORN
a modern version

1 quart dry yellow corn	2 tablespoons soda
2 quarts water	1 teaspoon salt

Soak corn overnight in the 2 quarts of water with soda. Boil in same water for about 3 hours, adding more water as needed. Drain, wash and rub off the hulls by hand. Boil again in fresh water. Drain again. Boil for 4 hours in fresh water with the salt. Serve hot with milk or butter.

CORN OYSTERS

2 cups fresh corn scraped from cob	1 teaspoon salt
	½ teaspoon pepper
2 eggs, well-beaten	2 tablespoons flour

Stir all together and drop by teaspoons into hot fat in a skillet or frying pan. Brown on one side, then turn once to brown on the other. Drain on absorbent paper and serve hot. Makes 8-10.

SUMMER SUCCOTASH

Many Plymouth people feel that the only dish deserving the name of Succotash is that noble chowder of hulled corn, dried beans, winter vegetables, etc., which is sacred to Forefathers' Day as turkey is to Thanksgiving. This is always called Plymouth Succotash. But it is the combination of corn and beans that makes Succotash. The Indians also used the term for the same dish of shell beans and green corn that is now often called Summer Succotash.

2 tablespoons butter	½ cup water
2 cups cooked beans	1 teaspoon salt
(Lima, shell, or kidney)	¼ teaspoon pepper
2 cups corn	1 teaspoon sugar
(scraped from cob)	¼ cup milk

Melt butter; add the beans, corn, and water, the seasonings and sugar. Cook over low heat. Stir in the milk as the water is absorbed. Heat thoroughly, but do not boil after milk is added. Serve very hot. 6 servings.

Spooner House 1760

THE SPOONER HOUSE, near the foot of old North Street, was built in the mid-eighteenth century and has remained in the Spooner family until the last owner, James Spooner, left it for use as a museum. In its pleasant interior are arranged the treasures of many generations of owners: fine old furniture, mirrors, family portraits, and china.

Life was considerably easier than in early Pilgrim days. Much entertaining was done, guests being invited for sumptuous dinners and teas.

Tea meant the evening meal and was served from a handsome tray with the best tea service set before the hostess. Many people have inherited large sets of china designed for such a meal: the tea service, cups and saucers, tea plates, three-inch butter plates, assorted platters and cake dishes and "sauce dishes" for the preserves.

Tea for the Evening
Scalloped Clams or Oysters
Cold Ham   Chicken for the Evening
Hot Bread or Rolls
Jellies   Relishes
Molded Dessert
or
Preserves
(home preserved in heavy syrup)
Cakes
(several kinds)

CHICKEN FOR THE EVENING

Boil a chicken in as little water as possible until the meat falls off the bones. Pick off the meat, season well with salt and pepper and put into a mold.

Boil down the water in which the chicken was cooked, until only a cup is left. Season well and pour over the chicken. It will sink through, forming a jelly around it. Chill well.

To serve, slice, and garnish the dish with celery.

Old Colony Club

The Old Colony Club has the pleasant distinction of being the oldest social club in continuous existence in this country. The club was founded in 1769 to provide a place where "pleasure and happiness . . . . of the respective members might be increased and to insure privacy not obtainable at the current public places."

Later in the year of 1769, the members voted to celebrate the landing of their forefathers at Plymouth. The first celebration occurred on December twenty-second.

This historic event started early in the morning with a discharge of cannon and the hoisting of the Club flag. At eleven o'clock the members assembled in the club and after a long social hour "a decent repast was set up."

Menu Served on First Forefathers' Day

December 22, 1769
from the records of the Old Colony Club

1) *A large baked Indian Whortleberry Pudding*
2) *A dish of Souquetash*
3) *A dish of Clamms*
4) *A dish of Oysters and a dish of Codfish*
5) *A haunch of venison roasted by the first*
   jack bro't to the Colony
6) *A dish of seafowl*
7) *A ditto of frost fish and Eeels*
8) *An apple Pye*
9) *A course of Cranberry Tarts and Cheese made*
   in the Old Colony

Dressed in the plainest manner (all appearance of luxury and extravagance being avoided, in imitation of our worthy ancestors whose memory we shall ever respect).

Pilgrim Society

The Pilgrim Society was organized in 1820, to insure a universal appreciation of the Pilgrims and their contribution to the American heritage. The Society maintains Pilgrim Hall as a museum and library, is responsible for the Forefathers' Monument and for Cole's Hill, which was the Pilgrim burial ground during their first precarious winter in Plymouth.

Pilgrim Society Dinner Menu

served August 1, 1899

Boiled Salmon with Green Peas

Roast Young Turkey   Roast Ribs of Beef

Mashed Potatoes   Green Peas   Sliced Tomatoes

Cucumber Pickles   Plain Gherkins   Lobster Salad

Vanilla Cream   Strawberry Cream   Chocolate Cream

Biscuit Glacé   Sherbet   Frozen Pudding

Almond Cake   Citron Cake   Currant Cake

Lady Cake   Macaroni Cake   Sponge Cake

Messina Oranges   Bananas

Tea   Coffee

Breads, Muffins, and Pancakes

White flour was a luxury in the early Pilgrim days. Some English wheat and rye were grown, and we find traces of their use in a group of receipts, such as Rye 'n' Injun Bread, and Brown Bread, both characteristic New England dishes.

Johnny Cake in all its forms developed from the cornmeal carried as provisions by Indian hunters. The name is probably a corruption of "Journey Cake."

Parched Indian corn was called Nokake. Roger Williams describes traveling through the woods with a group of Indians, "every man carrying a little basket of Nokake at his back, sufficient for a man three or four days. With a spoonful of this meal, and a spoonful of water from a brook, have I made many a good dinner and supper."

Pilgrim women learned from the Indians how to pound the corn in stone mortars, or in the hollowed part of a great log. Later a grist mill was established on the Town Brook in 1638 and a finer meal could be ground, usually used for bread or pudding.

John Josselyn, in NEW ENGLAND'S RARITIES DISCOVERED (1672), writes of corn thus: *"The English make a kind of Loblolly out of it, eat it with milk, which they call Samp. They beat it in* a mortar, and sift the flower out of it. The remainder they call Hominey, which they put into a pot of two or three gallons, with water, and boil it upon a gentle fire, till it be like Hasty Pudding. They put this in milk and so eat it.

"Their bread also they make of the hominey so boiled, and mix their flower with it, cast it into a deep basin in which they can form a loaf, and then turn it upon the peel, and presently put it into the oven before it spreads abroad.

"The flower makes excellent puddings."

INDIAN NOKAKE

Take very dry yellow field corn, preferably one or two years old, put it in a spider and brown it a light brown, stirring constantly over a low fire. It can then be ground to a fine powder in a coffee grinder. It used to be ground with mortar and pestle. It might take all day to do this, but a squaw's time was not valuable in those days. Sprinkled on ice cream or mixed in hot milk, it is a delicious and concentrated nourishment.

This receipt was given to the Harlow Old Fort House by a descendant of Chief Uncas of the Mohicans.

RYE 'N' INJUN BREAD
often called "Thirded Bread"

1 cup cormeal	3 tablespoons sugar
1 cup rye flour	1 teaspoon salt
1 cup flour	½ yeast cake in
1 cup milk, scalded	1 cup water

Blend meal and flours, add to milk after it has cooled. Add other ingredients and stir well. It will be stiff enough to shape. Knead well. Let rise until the top cracks open, then cut down, knead again, and shape into loaves. Put in buttered bread pan or pans, allow to rise to double its bulk. Bake in a moderate oven (350 F.) about 1 hour.

In the days of fireplace cookery, the dough was put into a bake kettle, which had been lined with green oak leaves. When the bread had risen for the second time, it was covered with more oak leaves, and the iron cover put in place. A bed of equal parts of embers and hot ashes was prepared, and the kettle set on it, and well heaped with more embers and hot ashes. Halfway through the baking, the top covering was raked off and renewed. If the under bed of coals was three or four inches thick, it would last through the baking. It took about one and a half hours to bake. Another method was to fill two large iron basins with the kneaded dough. Then, late in the evening, when the logs were well burned down, a space was cleared in the middle of the fireplace, and the basins were placed there, one on top of the other, so as to enclose their contents like one loaf. Then the ashes were added to completely cover and the bread left to bake until morning.

TO MAKE YEAST

1 cup grated raw potato	1 quart boiling water
1 cup sugar	½ cup salt

Pour the boiling water over the other ingredients. Let mixture stand until sufficiently fermented to use.

SQUASH BREAD

1 cup sieved cooked squash	1½ cups milk, scalded
1 teaspoon salt	½ yeast cake in
1 tablespoon butter	½ cup warm water
2 tablespoons sugar	4 cups flour

Combine all ingredients, mix well, turn out on floured board and knead about 15 minutes. Let rise in a bowl; when double in bulk, turn out on floured board and knead again, about 5 minutes. Shape into loaves, place in greased bread pans. Let rise to double its bulk and bake in a moderate oven (350 F.) about 1 hour. Makes 2 small loaves.

SQUASH MUFFINS

A Plymouth family receipt for Squash Muffins begins, "Take the squash that's left from dinner . . . " The modern way to make them would be to add ½ cup cooked squash to 2 cups of prepared muffin mix, and get a delicious variant of the usual muffin.

CORN CAKES

A receipt at least one hundred years old in the form quoted, much older in actual use:

Scald a quart of milk, pour it to three cups of Indian meal, add a bit of butter. When cool, stir in four eggs, a great spoonful of flour and a half teaspoon of salt. Bake in small cups for twenty minutes.

PILGRIM BANNOCK

2 cups milk	½ cup sugar
¾ cup white cornmeal	pinch salt
3 eggs	

Scald milk, pour over cornmeal, add sugar and salt. When cool, add beaten egg yolks, and fold in stiffly beaten egg whites. Bake in a shallow, greased baking pan in a moderate oven (350 F.) about 30 minutes.

The original Scotch bannock was a big scone baked in a griddle, like a large pancake, and made with barley, pea meal, or oatmeal. The Pilgrim adaptation called for corn meal. Sometimes molasses was used in place of sugar.

STEAMED BROWN BREAD

2 cups cornmeal	1 teaspoon soda in
2 cups rye meal	⅓ cup molasses
1 cup white flour	1½ cups cold water

Mix and sift dry ingredients, add soda, molasses, and water. Stir until well-mixed and fill well-greased mold not more than ⅔ full. Cover closely and place mold on trivet in kettle containing boiling water, allowing water to come halfway up around mold. Cover closely and steam 3-4 hours, adding boiling water as needed. Makes 2 quart molds.

Brown Bread is one of the earliest New England dishes, dating back to Plymouth Colony days. No doubt it was first boiled in a pudding cloth. The most meager Pilgrim household had at least a pot or kettle; brick ovens did not appear till permanent houses were built.

BROWN BREAD BREWIS

Cook dry Brown Bread slowly with a little cold water until soft. Add butter the size of a walnut. Serve as a breakfast or supper cereal, with cream and sugar.

RHODE ISLAND JOHNNY CAKE

"Take a sufficient quantity of meal, scald it, thin with a little cold milk, salt to taste."

This receipt appeared on a package of a brand of stone-ground white Rhode Island cornmeal much used in New Bedford (once part of Plymouth Colony). It was as explicit as the miller cared to make it, for his customers differed vigorously about the proper consistency of Johnny Cake. Some liked it thin as pancakes, others as thick as fish cakes. And how was he to know how many would be wanted?

Modern users know that the cornmeal should be covered with boiling water, left for about 10 minutes or until the meal swells about double in bulk. Thin to the consistency you desire, fry by spoonfuls on a hot griddle in butter for about 10 minutes, turning once. Serve with butter or maple syrup or with bacon.

JACKS

a traditional receipt from the southern part of the
Plymouth Colony

Break an egg into the cornmeal in your meal barrel. Add a cup of milk, a pinch of salt, and a pinch of soda. Mix in as much meal as the liquid will take up, and gather into balls. Fry in deep fat.

Gems for Breakfast

Gem pans were heavy cast-iron pans with rather shallow oblong divisions with rounded bottoms. A gem was rather like a small oblong popover. Sometimes they were made with rye flour instead of white flour. Gem pans were introduced to Plymouth kitchens about 100 years ago. They may still be found in antique shops. Home tinkerers like to keep nails in them.

PLYMOUTH GEMS

2 cups flour	1 cup water
1 cup milk	pinch salt

Mix all ingredients, beat well; pour into well-heated greased gem pans, and bake in a hot oven (400 F.) about 20 minutes. Eat immediately. Popover pans may be used, if desired. Fill pans only about ⅔ full.

RAISED RICE GEMS

1½ cups warm boiled rice	⅒ yeast cake in
1 cup flour	¼ cup warm water
½ cup scalded milk	1½ tablespoons butter
1 tablespoon sugar	1 egg

Stir rice, flour, milk, sugar, and yeast together well. Let stand overnight. In the morning, add butter, melted, and egg, stir briskly and mix well. Fill well-greased gem pans and let stand a few minutes in a warm place. Bake in a moderately hot oven (375 F.) about 20 minutes or until gems are a delicate brown. Makes 12 to 16 gems.

SALLY LUNN

1 yeast cake in	2 tablespoons butter, melted
2 cups lukewarm milk	½ teaspoon salt
1 cup light brown sugar	5 eggs
5½ cups flour (about)	

Dissolve yeast in milk, add sugar, butter, salt, and eggs, well-beaten. Add flour to make a soft batter. Let rise to double its bulk (about 2½ hours). Spoon into well-greased muffin pans and bake in a hot oven (400 F.) about 20 minutes.

HUCKLEBERRY PANCAKES

2¼ cups flour	1 tablespoon sugar
1 teaspoon baking powder	1 egg, beaten
⅛ teaspoon salt	2 cups milk
2 cups huckleberries	

Sift 2⅛ cups flour with baking powder, salt, and sugar. Beat egg with milk and add to flour mixture. Roll berries in remainder of flour and fold into batter. Bake on a hot, well-greased griddle. 1 tablespoon of the mixture makes 1 pancake. Makes about 24 cakes.

The Indians dry them (huckleberries and blueberries) in the sun and sell them to the English, who make use of them instead of currants, putting them in puddings, both boiled and baked.

NEW ENGLAND'S RARITIES DISCOVERED
John Josselyn (1672)

HASTY PUDDING

6 cups boiling water	1 teaspoon salt
1 cup yellow cornmeal	

Bring water to a rapid boil, add salt. Slowly stir in cornmeal, stirring constantly, until mixture is smooth. Set over hot water and steam about 30 minutes. Serve hot with molasses or milk, or sugar and butter and nutmeg. 8 servings.

Place leftover mush in a bread pan that has been rinsed with cold water. When cold, the mush can then be sliced, the slices dusted lightly with flour and fried on a hot griddle. Serve with molasses or with butter and maple syrup.

SOUR MILK PANCAKES

2½ cups flour	1¼ teaspoons baking powder
½ teaspoon salt	2 cups sour or buttermilk
1 teaspoon soda	1 egg

Mix and sift flour, salt, soda and baking powder. Add sour or buttermilk and egg. Beat well and drop by spoonfuls on a hot greased griddle. Turn once to brown on other side. Serve with butter and maple syrup. Makes 12-15 cakes.

DUXBURY RUSKS

2⅛ cups flour, sifted	1 teaspoon cloves
1 teaspoon soda	1 cup sugar
½ teaspoon salt	½ cup shortening
1 teaspoon nutmeg	1 egg, beaten
1 teaspoon cinnamon	1 cup sour milk

½ cup raisins

Mix and sift dry ingredients; cream sugar and shortening. Add egg and stir in milk and dry ingredients, alternately. Stir in raisins. Pour into a well-greased square baking tin and bake in a moderate oven (350 F.) 1 hour. Cut in squares to serve.

CRANBERRY DROP CAKES

2 cups cranberries	1¼ tablespoons melted butter
½ cup water	½ teaspoon salt
½ cup sugar	dash cinnamon

1 cup cracker crumbs

Wash and pick over cranberries, add water and cook until berries are soft. Force through a sieve, add sugar to pulp and then add butter and seasonings. Stir in cracker crumbs. Drop by spoonfuls into deep hot fat (370 F.) and cook until browned. Drain and serve hot or cold. These were often served with chicken or turkey in place of potatoes. 6 servings.

Cookies and Cakes

There being no sugar cane in that country, those trees (maples) supplied that liquor, which being boiled up and evaporated turned to a kind of sugar somewhat brownish but very good.

Joutel (1687)

SMALL SEED CAKES
a 1700 receipt

Take one pound of sugar and as much flour; a pound of butter washed in rose water, drean out the rose water. Four eggs and a few drops of oyl of sinnamont and a good hanfull of carraway seeds. Bruse them all a little. Mix all together then drop them in lumps as big as nutmegs upon buttered paper. Bake them in a crisp oven. Then dry them on a dish till crisp.

Nowadays, instead of using rose water, one might use one half teaspoon of rose extract mixed with a little water.

MOLASSES COOKIES

2 cups shortening	2 teaspoons soda
1 cup sugar	2 teaspoons ginger
2 cups molasses	flour
1 cup water	½ pound currants or
1 teaspoon powdered alum	raisins, chopped

Cream shortening and sugar, add molasses and water. Sift alum, soda, and ginger with about 2 cups of flour and stir into first mixture. Add fruit. Add more flour, if necessary, to make mixture stiff enough to handle. Chill and roll out on floured board. Cut and bake in a moderately hot oven (375 F.) about 10 minutes.

SCHOOLBOY COOKIES

Make like Molasses Cookies, but add 1 teaspoon cinnamon.

GRANDMOTHER'S HERMITS

2 cups sugar	1 teaspoon each of cinnamon,
1 cup butter	clove, nutmeg, allspice, and
yolks of 3 eggs	ginger
3½ cups flour	white of 1 egg
1 teaspoon soda dissolved	sugar
in 1 tablespoon milk	

Cream sugar and butter, add egg yolks. Sift flour with spices and add to first mixture. Add extra flour, if necessary, to make dough stiff enough to handle. Chill, roll out on floured board. Cut and bake in a moderate oven (350 F.) about 15 minutes. As soon as cookies are removed from oven, brush with white of egg and sprinkle with sugar.

CARAWAY COOKIES

1 cup sugar	1 teaspoon salt
½ cup butter	1 teaspoon cream of tartar
2 eggs	½ teaspoon soda
1½ cups flour	1½ teaspoons caraway seeds

Cream together the sugar and butter, add eggs. Sift flour with salt, cream of tartar and soda, add to first mixture, and add seeds. Roll out on a floured board and cut in rounds. Bake in a moderately hot oven (375 F.) about 12 minutes. Makes 16-20 cookies.

Gingerbread was a prime favorite in early New England days and still is. Receipts are as numerous as those for Johnny Cake or cornbread. The only thing most cooks seem to agree upon is that, like Chaucer, they find gingerbread to be "full fair."

MAPLE SYRUP GINGERBREAD

2 cups flour	1 teaspoon ginger
1 teaspoon soda	1 egg, beaten
½ teaspoon salt	1 cup sour cream

1 cup maple syrup

Combine the flour, soda, salt, and ginger. Mix egg, sour cream, and syrup and combine mixtures. Bake in a buttered cake pan in a moderate oven (350 F.) about 40 minutes.

SUGAR GINGERBREAD
from an old notebook

Rub one-half pound of butter and one pound of sugar together, add six well-beaten eggs, then one pound of flour and two table-spoons ginger, sifted together. Bake in two square tin sheets for forty minutes in a mild oven.

MOLASSES GINGERBREAD

½ cup shortening	½ teaspoon salt
½ cup sugar	1½ teaspoons soda
1 cup molasses	1 teaspoon cinnamon
1 egg, beaten	1 teaspoon ginger
2 cups flour	½ teaspoon cloves

1 cup hot water

Mix shortening, sugar, molasses, and egg. Sift dry ingredients, and add to first mixture. Then add the hot water and stir until smooth. Bake in a greased cake pan in a moderate oven (350 F.) for about 35 minutes.

MUSTER GINGERBREAD

Muster Gingerbread was made and sold in the old days at "Musters," the drill period for the volunteer soldiers, and an exciting time in country places.

3 cups flour	1 cup molasses
1 teaspoon salt	1 cup sugar
2 teaspoons soda	1 cup sour milk
2 teaspoons ginger	1 cup shortening

Sift dry ingredients. Combine molasses, sugar, and sour milk, add shortening, melted. Combine two mixtures and add more flour, if necessary, to make a dough stiff enough to handle. Roll out on a floured board, a little thicker than for cookies, cut in strips, and bake in a hot oven (400 F.) about 10-12 minutes. Makes 30 cookies.

REAL STRAWBERRY SHORTCAKE

2 cups flour	¾ cup milk
4 teaspoons baking powder	melted butter
½ teaspoon salt	strawberries, crushed and
4 tablespoons butter	sweetened

Sift dry ingredients, work in butter as for pastry, add milk. Turn on a floured board and divide into 2 parts. Roll out. Place one in buttered pie plate; spread with melted butter; and place second round on top. Bake in a hot oven (400 F.) about 15-20 minutes. Do not allow to get too brown.

Separate crusts, butter well, and place between and on top ripe strawberries, crushed and sweetened to taste. 6 servings.

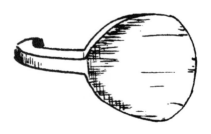

A member of an old Plymouth family said that on Election Day all the country cousins came to Plymouth to vote and then came to her mother's house on North Street for dinner. Often there were twenty or more. Election Cake was made for just such occasions. An old receipt calls for thirty quarts of flour, a quart of yeast, fourteen pounds of sugar, a dozen eggs, a quart of brandy, ten pounds of butter, twelve pounds of raisins, and other ingredients in like proportions. Here is a more modern adaptation of that ancient receipt.

ELECTION CAKE

2 cups raised light dough	1 teaspoon soda in
1 cup butter	1 tablespoon warm water
2 cups sugar	1 cup raisins
3 eggs	1 whole nutmeg, grated

Knead dough slightly on floured board. Cream butter and sugar, add eggs, beaten, and beat again. Work into the dough until soft. Add soda, chopped and floured raisins, and grated nutmeg. Shape into loaves, place in well-greased bread pans or 2 loaves in a large oblong pan; let rise until double in bulk; and bake in a moderate oven (350 F.) about 1 hour.

BRIDE'S CAKE
an 1870 receipt

3 cups sifted flour	2 cups sugar
5 tablespoons baking powder	½ teaspoon rose extract
½ teaspoon salt	½ teaspoon almond extract
1 cup butter	1 cup milk
6 egg whites	

Sift flour, baking powder, and salt 3 times. Cream butter and sugar well. Add extracts to milk and add milk and flour mixtures to creamed mixture alternately, beating well after each addition. Beat egg whites until stiff and fold in carefully. Turn into a greased 10-inch tube pan and bake in a moderate oven (350 F.) about 1½ hours.

GROOM'S CAKE
an 1883 receipt

2 cups butter	4½ cups flour
1 pound package light brown sugar	2 teaspoons cinnamon
	1 tablespoon nutmeg
16–18 eggs (2 cups)	1 tablespoon allspice
½ cup heavy sweet cream	2 pounds each of currants, seeded raisins, chopped, and Sultana raisins
1 cup brandy	
1 tablespoon orange flower water	
1½ pounds citron	1½ cups shaved almonds or other nuts

Cream butter with sugar well. Beat eggs until light and frothy and add to creamed mixture. Then add liquids. Sift flour with spices and sift again over fruit. Blend two mixtures and fill 9-inch square pans nearly to top, lined with buttered and floured paper. Bake in a moderate oven (350 F.) about 1 hour. Let cool in pans and ice with boiled white icing. Makes 2 cakes.

CITRON CAKE
from Mary B. Combes' manuscript notebook — 1843

Two cups dried apples, cut coarsely, and soaked. Drain off all the water, add two cups of molasses, and boil about an hour. Then add one cup of milk, one-half cup butter, two teaspoons soda, one teaspoon cream of tartar, five cups of flour, spice to taste. A little spice improves flavor.

SAFFRON CAKE

2 cups milk
1 cup sugar
1 cup butter
½ teaspoon salt
1 yeast cake in
¼ cup warm water
1 teaspoon saffron in
1 teaspoon warm milk
3 eggs, beaten
4 cups flour
1 teaspoon each cloves and mace
½ teaspoon cinnamon
2 cups currants, washed

Scald and cool milk and pour over sugar, butter, and salt. When lukewarm, add yeast and saffron juice, eggs, flour, spices, and currants. Beat well and let rise to double its bulk. Cut down, put in a greased pan and let rise again until light. Bake in moderate oven (350 F.) about 1 hour.

TO MAKE LITTLE CAKES FOR TEA
a 1756 receipt

Of butter, flower, sugar, a quarter of a pound of each and as much yoke of egg as will mix into a stiff paste. Make them into round cakes the size of half a crown. Bake them in tins. Put some carraway seeds in them.

SPONGE CAKE

6 eggs
3 cups sugar
2 teaspoons cream of tartar
2 cups pastry flour
1 teaspoon soda in
1 cup water
grated rind of 1 lemon
juice of half a lemon
¼ teaspoon salt
2 cups flour, additional

Beat eggs for 2 minutes, add sugar and beat for 5 minutes. Sift cream of tartar with flour and add to first mixture. Beat 2 minutes, add soda to water and add to mixture; beat 1 minute. Then add all the rest of ingredients and beat all 1 minute more. Bake in large ungreased tube pan in a moderate oven (350 F.) about 1 hour.

TO ICE A GREAT CAKE

from THE ART OF COOKING MADE PLAIN AND EASY,
H. Glasse, Edinburgh, Scotland (1791)

Take the whites of twenty-four eggs, a pound of double-refined sugar, beat and sifted fine; mix both together in a deep earthenware pan and with a whisk, whisk it well for two or three hours together till it looks white and thick, then with a broad board or bunch of feathers spread it all over the top and sides of the cake.

Set it at a proper distance before a good clear fire and keep turning it continually for fear of its changing color; but a cool oven is best and an hour hardens it.

You may perfume the icing with what perfume you prefer.

SOUR APPLE CAKE

1 cup sugar	1 cup sour apple sauce
½ cup shortening	1¾ cups flour
¼ teaspoon salt	½ teaspoon each cloves,
1 teaspoon baking soda in	nutmeg
¼ cup warm water	1 teaspoon cinnamon

1   cup raisins

Cream together sugar, shortening and salt. Add soda in water to apple sauce. Combine mixtures and let foam. Sift flour with spices and add to foamy mixture; fold in raisins. Bake in a greased loaf pan in a moderate oven (350 F.) about 45 minutes.

ONE-TWO-THREE-FOUR CAKE
from THE TRIP-HAMMER COOK BOOK
Kingston (1894)

1 cup butter	4 eggs
2 cups sugar	1 teaspoon vanilla
3 cups flour	2 teaspoons baking powder

Cream butter and sugar, add eggs, beaten well, and flavoring (any flavoring desired may be used). Sift flour and baking powder and combine with first mixture. Bake in a large oblong greased baking pan in a moderate oven (350 F.) about 35 to 45 minutes.

BURLINGTON LOVE KNOTS
from the IMPROVED HOUSEWIFE, Mrs. A. L. Webster (1863)

Take three eggs, five spoonfuls of white sugar, half teaspoonful of saleratus dissolved in two spoonfuls of cold water, half-egg-size of butter and flour enough to roll. Cut the sheet in slips, tie them in love knots and fry in pure white lard.

BLUEBERRY CAKE

1½ cups sugar	¼ teaspoon salt
2 eggs	1 tablespoon butter, melted
2 cups flour	½ cup milk
2 teaspoons baking powder	2 cups floured blueberries

Beat sugar and eggs, add flour sifted with baking powder and salt, butter and milk. Add blueberries last. Bake in greased square pan in a moderate oven (350 F.) about 30-35 minutes.

... there is gooseberries, bilberries, Treakleberries, Hustleberries, Currents, which being dryed in the sunne are a little inferior to those that our Grocers sell in England.

NEW ENGLAND'S PROSPECT,
William Wood (1634)

AUNT HATTIE'S LEMON - JELLY CAKE

1 cup sugar	½ teaspoon soda
½ cup butter	1 teaspoon cream of tartar
1 egg	2⅓ cups flour
	⅔ cup milk

Cream sugar and butter, add eggs. Sift soda, cream of tartar with flour and add alternately with milk to creamed mixture. Bake in 2 greased round cake pans, in a moderate oven (350 F.) about 25-30 minutes.

LEMON JELLY FILLING

2 lemons	2 egg yolks
1 cup sugar	2 tablespoons butter

Use juice and grated rind of lemon. Combine all ingredients and bring to a boil, then cool.

LEMON JELLY FROSTING

1 egg white	powdered sugar
1 tablespoon cream	shredded coconut

Beat egg white until stiff, add cream and enough sugar to make of spreading consistency. Add shredded coconut, if desired, to the icing but reserve some for top of cake. Cover a layer of cake with the lemon jelly filling, then cover that with frosting and sprinkle with coconut. Then add second layer, more lemon filling, and top with frosting, and sprinkle with coconut.

DELICIOUS GOLD CAKE

½ cup butter	½ cup milk
1 cup sugar	1½ cups flour
yolks of 8 eggs	2 teaspoons baking powder

Cream butter and sugar well. Beat egg yolks to a stiff froth and stir into butter mixture. Add milk, and flour and baking powder, sifted together. Beat well. Turn into a greased tube pan and bake in a moderate oven (350 F.) about 1 hour.

Pies and Puddings

"Ah, on Thanksgiving Day when from East and from West,
From North and from South come the pilgrim and guest,
When the grey-haired New Englander sees round his board,
The old broken links of affection restored,
When the care wearied man seeks his mother once more,
And the worn matron smiles where the girl smiled before,
What moistens the lip and what brightens the eye?
What calls back the past like the rich Pumpkin Pie?"

The Pumpkin, John Greenleaf Whittier (1850)

PUMPKIN PIE

1 cup granulated sugar	½ teaspoon cloves
½ teaspoon salt	½ teaspoon ginger
1½ teaspoons cinnamon	½ teaspoon allspice
½ teaspoon nutmeg	1⅔ cups evaporated milk
1½ cups canned pumpkin	

Mix all together, pour into pastry-lined pie plate. Bake in hot oven (400 F.) about 10 minutes, then reduce heat to moderate (350 F.) and bake about 30-35 minutes or until a silver knife inserted in center comes out clean. 1 large pie.

SQUASH PIE

1 cup sugar	½ teaspoon ginger or nutmeg
3 eggs, beaten	¼ teaspoon cinnamon
pinch of salt	1¾ cups milk
1 cup cooked squash	

Mix all together, pour into pastry-lined pie plate. Bake in a hot oven (400 F.) about 10 minutes, then reduce heat to moderate (350 F.) and bake about 25-30 minutes longer or until a silver knife inserted in center comes out clean. 1 pie.

MARLBOROUGH PIES

from an old Plymouth manuscript notebook

Mix together one quart of strained sour apples, one quart of sugar, eight eggs, one pint of cream and one-quarter pound of butter, the juice, pulp and grated rind of one lemon and three nutmegs, grated. Make individual open pies (pies in one crust).

FRIED PIES

2 cups flour	1 egg, beaten
1 teaspoon baking powder	milk to make a soft dough
3–4 tablespoons lard or other shortening	dried apple sauce

Sift flour with baking powder, blend in shortening as for pastry, add egg and just enough milk to make a soft dough. Divide dough into 15 small pieces. Roll out each piece, put a spoonful of apple sauce in the middle and fold edges over, pressing together tightly. Drop into deep fat (385 F.) and fry until golden brown, turning once.

GRANDMOTHER'S MINCEMEAT

1 pound each	1 pound orange peel
currants	½ pound citron
seedless raisins	5 lemons
seeded raisins	1 teaspoon each
suet	allspice
sugar	nutmeg
apples	lemon, almond, and vanilla
lemon peel	flavoring

Wash fruit, and chop with rest of ingredients; mix well in a large bowl. Put in sterilized jars and seal.

Grandmother kept her mincemeat in a crock, and it kept for a long time.

Sometimes venison was used in mincemeat. The best part to use was meat from the forequarter. When meat is used, the mincemeat must be cooked before sealing in jars.

WILD CHOKECHERRIES

The cherry tree yields a great store of cherries, which grow on clusters like grapes; they be much smaller than our English cherries; nothing neare so good if they be not very ripe; they so furre the mouth that the tongue will cleave to the roofe, and the throat was horse with swallowing those red berries, as I may call them, being little better in taste.

New England's Prospect,
William Wood (1634)

RIPE CHERRY PIE

Rich, ripe cherries are required for this pie. Wild chokecherries will not do!

Line a deep pie plate with a rich pastry crust. Stone cherries, enough to fill the pie, heaping them in the center and sprinkling ½ cup of sugar over them. Cover with pastry, prick top with a fork, and bake in hot oven (400 F.) until crust is golden brown (about 25-30 minutes). If crust browns too quickly, reduce heat to moderate (350 F.) for last part of baking.

BLUEBERRY PIE

2½ cups blueberries   1 cup sugar
flour   ½ teaspoon salt
pastry for 2 crusts

Line a deep pie plate with pastry, fill with berries lightly dredged with flour, sprinkled with sugar and salt. Cover with pastry, prick top with a fork, and bake in a hot oven (400 F.) about ten minutes, then reduce heat to moderate (350 F.) and continue baking about 30 minutes. Makes 1 large pie.

RHUBARB PIE

rhubarb   1 egg
1 cup sugar   ½ teaspoon salt
pastry for 2 crusts

Cut up enough rhubarb to fill a pie plate (about 3 cups), cover with sugar and salt, stir in egg and mix thoroughly. Fill a pastry-lined pie plate, cover with crust and prick top well. Bake in hot oven (400 F.) about 10 minutes; reduce heat to moderate (350 F.) and continue baking about 30 minutes. Makes 1 large pie.

FOUR BERRY PUDDING

Stew any four kinds of berries, such as raspberries, blackberries, blueberries, and currants, with a little water and sweeten to taste. Butter slices of stale bread and put one layer, butter side down, in a deep dish. Dip on fruit until all is saturated, repeat. Be sure no bread shows. Chill well, serve with cream.

ENGLISH BOILED PUDDING

2 cups flour	1 teaspoon salt
2 teaspoons baking powder	milk
¼ cup sugar	apples or other fruit

Sift together flour, baking powder, sugar, and salt, wet with milk until about as stiff as pie crust. Roll out on a floured board, using plenty of flour until about ½ inch thick and oval in shape. Place prepared fruit, such as cut-up apples, in center of oval and press into the dough. Roll like a jelly roll, wet ends and press wet edges together. Lay on a well-floured cloth, roll up and tie the ends, leaving room for it to swell. Place in a large kettle of boiling water, cover and boil without removing cover for an hour. Serve with pudding sauce.

QUEEN OF PUDDINGS

2 cups fine bread crumbs	2 cups sugar
4 cups milk	1 lemon
4 eggs	2–3 tablespoons butter
jelly	

Soak bread in milk until soft, add egg yolks, beaten with 1 cup sugar, grated rind of lemon, and butter. Bake in a buttered cake pan in a moderate oven (350 F.) about 1 hour. Remove from oven, spread with jelly, then with a mixture of egg whites, beaten stiff with 1 cup sugar and juice of lemon. Bake in a moderate oven about 15 minutes to brown the topping. Good hot or cold. 8-10 servings.

BRADFORD PLUM PUDDING

Governor William Bradford of Plymouth married Alice South-worth, who came to Plymouth in the ship "Anne" in 1623. She set a good table and made a plum pudding that became famous. She probably used maple syrup, dried grapes, and candied melons and cherries she'd made herself.

1 pound buttered bread	1 cup seeded raisins
3 cups milk, scalded	1 cup seedless raisins
5 eggs	1 cup currants
1 cup dark molasses	½ cup citron, shaved thin
1 teaspoon salt	½ cup candied cherries, halved

3 cups cold milk

Slice and butter the bread and cover with scalded milk, let stand for 15 minutes. Mash with fork, after removing the crusts. Add eggs, beaten, molasses, and salt and then the fruit. Butter a large pudding mold or bread pan and pour in the mixture, to within 2 inches of the top. Set in a pan of hot water and bake for several hours in a moderate oven (350 F.). As the crust forms, gash with a knife and pour in milk, one cup at a time. When a silver knife inserted in the center comes out clean, the pudding is done. Keep in the mold until ready to serve. 8-10 servings.

INDIAN PUDDING

4 cups milk	2 or 3 eggs
½ cup cornmeal	1 teaspoon ginger
1 cup dark molasses	1 teaspoon salt

2 tablespoons butter

Scald milk, stir in cornmeal, add molasses, eggs, ginger, and salt. Dot with butter. Bake in a buttered pudding dish in a slow oven (300 F.) about 2 hours. Serve hot or cold with cream.

An old Plymouth Colony receipt says: "Take the morning's milk and throw into it as much cornmeal as you can hold in the palm of your hand. Let the molasses drip in as you sing 'Nearer My God to Thee,' but sing two verses in cold weather."

POOR MAN'S PUDDING

4 cups milk
½ cup raw rice
½ teaspoon salt
1 tablespoon sugar

Mix all together, pour into a buttered pudding dish, and bake in a slow oven (300 F.) for 2 hours. 6-8 servings.

KATIE'S RICE PUDDING

½ cup rice
½ teaspoon salt
1 lemon
1 cup milk
2 eggs
2 tablespoons butter
1 cup sugar

Boil rice until soft, add salt. Add grated lemon rind, milk, and egg yolks and butter. Mix all together and bake in a greased pudding dish or casserole in a moderate oven (350 F.) about 35 minutes. Remove from oven and cover with a meringue made with the egg whites beaten stiff with a cup of sugar and juice of half the lemon. Return to oven to brown meringue (about 15-20 minutes).

GRANDFATHER'S CORNMEAL PUDDING

¾ cup cornmeal
1¼ cups flour
¼ cup sugar
4 teaspoons baking powder
½ teaspoon salt
1 cup milk
1 tablespoon butter
1 egg, beaten

Sift dry ingredients, add rest of ingredients, and pour into 2 greased brown bread molds, cover tightly, and steam over boiling water about ½ hour. Serve with boiled and cooled molasses and ice-cold sour cream. Makes 2 large loaves.

APPLE DUMPLINGS

Pare and core apples. Set each apple on a square of pastry. Fill center of apple with a mixture of raisins and brown sugar, and wrap pastry round apple, being careful to seal edges. Bake in a moderately hot oven (375 F.) until apple is soft when tested with a fork. Serve with cream or sauce.

APPLE PAN DOWDY

from an old manuscript notebook, dated 1800

Fill a baking-dish or an old-fashioned bean pot full of sliced apples. Add:

1 cup molasses
1 cup sugar
1 cup water

1 teaspoon cloves
1 teaspoon cinnamon

Cover with baking powder biscuit crust, lapping it over the sides. Bake overnight. Cut the hard crust into the apples when serving. Serve with cream.

BROWN BETTY PUDDING

from an old manuscript notebook

Put a layer of tart apple slices in the bottom of a pudding dish, with sugar and other seasonings to taste, then a layer of bread crumbs. Repeat alternate layers until full. Bake about two hours.

APPLE TAPIOCA

⅓ cup minute tapioca
½ cup sugar
½ teaspoon salt
2 cups boiling water

3 large apples, sliced and
    quartered
sprinkle of cinnamon and
    nutmeg
butter

Mix tapioca, sugar, salt, and water and cook in top of double boiler over hot water until thickened. Add apples and cook until apples are soft. Place in a buttered baking dish, sprinkle with spices and butter. Put under broiler to brown. Serve hot with cream.

CHOCOLATE BLANC MANGE

4 cups milk
½ cup Irish moss
    (well-washed)
½ cup water

1½ ounces unsweetened
    chocolate
½ cup sugar
1 teaspoon vanilla

Cook milk, moss, and water together ½ hour, strain into a bowl. Heat other ingredients over hot water until chocolate is melted, add to milk mixture. Cool before serving. 6-8 servings.

GOOSEBERRY FOOL

1 quart gooseberries	¼ teaspoon salt
2 cups water	4 eggs
1 cup sugar	2 tablespoons powdered sugar
1 tablespoon butter	

Top and stem berries and stew in water until tender. Press through a sieve, add sugar, butter, salt, and egg yolks, well beaten. Pour into a bowl. Beat egg whites until stiff with powdered sugar. Pour over first mixture in bowl. Serve cold. 4-6 servings.

NOTTINGHAM PUDDING
from an old manuscript notebook

Peel and core six apples and fill cavities with sugar; place in pye-dish and pour over it a nice light batter, prepared as for batter pudding and bake one hour in a moderate oven.

BLUEBERRY PUDDING

1 quart blueberries	½ teaspoon salt
1 cup sugar	1 teaspoon cinnamon
½ cup water	1 slice stale bread, buttered

Boil all ingredients, except bread, together for a few minutes. Pour this over the bread which has been cut in thirds and placed in a baking dish. Cover and let stand at least 1 hour. Serve with cream. 6 servings.

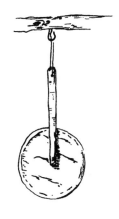

DR. ZABDIEL BOYLSTON'S
HONEYCOMB PUDDING

The good doctor was the one who introduced smallpox inoculation into Boston. Perhaps this pudding gave him the necessary courage. He needed it, as he was almost mobbed on several occasions.

½ cup flour	½ cup butter, melted
½ cup sugar	½ cup warm milk
½ teaspoon each clove, cinnamon, and allspice	4 eggs, beaten
	1 tablespoon soda in
¼ teaspoon salt	1 cup molasses

Stir together all dry ingredients, add rest of ingredients, and pour quickly into a buttered baking dish. Bake in a moderate oven (350 F.) about 30 minutes. Turn out on a hot plate. When sliced the honeycomb will show. Serve with Honeycomb Pudding Sauce.

HONEYCOMB PUDDING SAUCE

1 cup sugar	¼ teaspoon salt
¼ cup butter	2 teaspoons cornstarch
juice of 1 lemon	1 cup boiling water
1 egg, beaten	

Cream sugar and butter, add rest of ingredients, and cook over low heat, stirring constantly, until thickened.

A TANSY PUDDING
from a sixteenth century cook book

Blanch and pound a quarter of a pound of Jordan almonds. Put them in a stew pan, add a gill of syrup of Rose, the crumbs of a French roll, some grated nutmeg, half a glass of brandy, two tablespoonfuls of tansy juice, three ounces of fresh butter and some slices of citron. Sweeten and mix it, when cold add the juice of a lemon and eight eggs beaten. It may be either boyled or baked.

HARD SAUCE

1 cup powdered sugar	1 egg white
½ cup butter	flavoring as desired

Rub sugar and butter together, fold in stiffly beaten egg white. Flavor to taste. Serve on hot puddings.

LEMON SAUCE

3 tablespoons cornstarch	2 cups boiling water
1 cup sugar	1 lemon
	1 tablespoon butter

Mix cornstarch and sugar, add boiling water and cook, stirring constantly, until thickened, or about 10 minutes. Add the grated rind and juice of the lemon and the butter. If sauce is too thick to pour, add more boiling water.

FAVORITE PUDDING SAUCES
from an old manuscript notebook

Cold Sauce; one cup of butter, two cups of sugar well creamed together and flavored. Delicious on apple pudding.

Egg Sauce; with an egg-beater, beat three eggs until they are thick or beat yolks and whites separately and afterwards mix them. Then beat well in one large cup of sugar, flavor it and serve as soon as made. This is very fine.

Molasses Sauce; one cup of molasses, small piece of butter, one tablespoon vinegar, boil together ten minutes. Good on apple pudding.

Another; one cup of sugar, a little butter, one egg, beaten together, stir in one half cup of hot water, set it in a pan of hot water and boil it five minutes.

Antiquarian House
1809

THE ANTIQUARIAN HOUSE, built in 1809, is distinguished by its delicate proportions, and interesting octagonal rooms, its graceful furniture and household appointments. The house is maintained and opened to the public by the members of the Antiquarian Society, a woman's organization, dedicated to the Pilgrim women.

Every member of the Society is deeply conscious of the great contribution made to this New World by the Pilgrim women. When the passengers on the Mayflower crossed the Atlantic Ocean, they came with the fixed purpose of establishing, not a transient colony, but permanent homes here in America.

Women held the welfare of the "New Plimoth" in their capable hands; they made hearths glow and candles shine; they fed and clothed and upheld their families, nursed the sick and encouraged the downhearted. They bore and reared their children to become the pioneers of a new nation. This was a heroic task. Three thousand miles of tossing ocean lay between them and their familiar household things. On the crowded ship they could bring only a few pots, a chest, a chair, perhaps a spinning wheel, the garden seeds cherished from well-ordered Dutch and English gardens. They came into a bleak and sparse land, deserted Indian cornfields and an almost unbroken forest.

Pilgrim women made a notable success of this undertaking, using their skills and commonsense as housewives to adapt to new conditions, always upheld by deep devotion to the cause for which they had left their old homes forever. These staunch Pilgrim women must, indeed, be given full credit for their share in establishing the permanent settlement of Plymouth Colony.

PLIMOTH PLANTATION was founded a few years ago to reaffirm its members' belief in the fundamentals of the Pilgrim heritage. To re-create a dramatic chapter of history, Plimoth Plantation is building again at its hundred-acre site on Eel River, Plymouth, Massachusetts, the first Pilgrim village and the berthing place for the Mayflower II. This, it is hoped, will build for America, a living monument to the men and women whose courageous devotion to individual liberties, helped to found our nation.

As Samuel Eliot Morison has written, ". . . Here is the story of a simple people impelled by an ardent faith in God to a dauntless courage in danger, a boundless resourcefulness in the face of difficulty, an impregnable fortitude in adversity. It strengthens and inspires us all, after more than three centuries, in this age of change and uncertainty. . . . The story of their patience and fortitude, and the workings of that unseen force which bears up heroic souls in the doings of mighty errands, as often as it is read or told, quickens the spiritual forces in American life, strengthens faith in God, and confidence in human nature. Thus the Pilgrims in a sense have become the spiritual ancestors of all Americans, whatever their stock, race or creed."

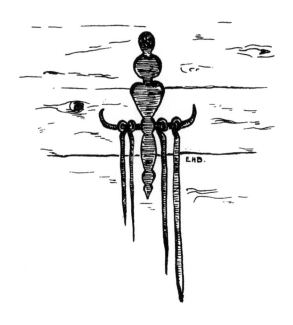

Plymouth Curiosities

Cran Berry or Bearberry, because the bears use much to feed upon them, is a small trayling plant that grows in salt marshes that are overgrown with moss. The Berries are of a pale yellow color after-ward red, as big as a cherry; some perfectly round, others oval; all of them hollow with a sower astringent taste; they are ripe in August and September.

The Indians and English use them much boyling them with Sugar for Sauce to eat with their meat; and it is a delicate Sauce, especially for roasted Mutton; Some make tarts with them as with Goose Berries.

NEW ENGLAND'S RARITIES DISCOVERED
John Josselyn (1672)

PLYMOUTH CRANBERRY PIE

3 to 4 cups cranberries	1 egg
1 cup sugar	½ teaspoon almond extract

pastry for 2 crusts

Chop cranberries, mix with sugar, egg, and extract. Place in a pastry-lined pie plate, cover with lattice strips of pastry and seal edges. Bake in a hot oven (400 F.) about 10 minutes, then reduce heat to moderate (350 F.) and continue baking about 35 minutes or until cranberries are soft and pastry is browned.

Another version of Cranberry Pie is made by boiling 4 cups of cranberries with 2 cups of boiling water for 20 minutes; then straining the sauce and adding 2 cups of sugar. Boil for 5 minutes longer. While still hot turn into pastry-lined pie plate, cover with crust or lattice strips and bake as for Plymouth Cranberry Pie, only until crust is well-browned, about 15-20 minutes.

CANDIED CRANBERRIES

2 cups cranberries	½ teaspoon salt
2 cups sugar	¼ teaspoon soda
1 cup cold water	

Put all ingredients in large kettle, cover tightly, and boil for 15 minutes. Do not remove cover while boiling or until it is perfectly cold.

CRANBERRY JELLY

1 quart cranberries	2 cups sugar
2 cups water	

Boil cranberries in the water for 10 minutes, strain, and add the sugar; boil for 10 minutes longer. Skim, and pour into sterilized jelly glasses. Cover with paraffin.

CRANBERRY JUICE

Pick over and wash cranberries. Put in a large kettle and add water until it shows through the fruit. Cook until soft. Strain through jelly bag, measure and add 1 cup sugar for each 3 cups fruit juice. Boil 15 minutes and pour into sterilized jars and seal tightly. The juice will probably need to be diluted for serving.

CRANBERRY JUICE COCKTAIL

1 quart cranberries	2 cups boiling water
2 cups sugar	fresh herb bouquet

Boil berries, sugar, and water together until berries are soft, strain. Add a fresh herb bouquet of Lemon Thyme, Lemon Balm, Hyssop, and Burnet. Boil 5 minutes longer, remove herbs and chill.

Some Old Time Beverages
MINT TEA

Put several sprigs of mint in the pot with the tea and pour boiling water over. Strain and serve with a leaf or two of mint and a slice of lemon in the cup.

SWITCHEL OR SWIZZLE

It was considered dangerous for overheated hay-makers to drink large quantities of water; so either raw oatmeal was added to the water, or molasses, vinegar, and ginger. To 1 gallon of water, add 3 cups molasses, 1 cup vinegar, and 1 teaspoon ginger. These proportions may be altered to suit individual tastes.

ELDER BLOSSOM WINE
from a 1700 English receipt

1 pint elder blossoms tightly packed	2 yeast cakes
	3 pounds raisins
9 pounds sugar	3 gallons boiling water

Put blossoms in covered stone jar. Let stand until you can shake off blossoms but not long enough for them to turn black. Add sugar and pour over boiling water. When lukewarm, add yeast cakes. Let stand 5 days, turning once or twice a day. Chop raisins and add. Let work. About January or February strain and bottle.

WILD CHERRY BRANDY

Fill a glass gallon jar three-quarters full of dead ripe wild cherries (or chokecherries). Cover with boiled syrup so thick that it is sticky between the fingers. Add 1 quart of pure grain alcohol. Cover tightly and don't open till Christmas!

ELDERBERRY WINE

Put berries in a tub, cover with water. Crush and continue crushing as berries rise to the surface.

After 7 days, strain off juice and measure. To every 2 quarts of juice, add 1 quart water. Put in kegs or barrels and keep filled up with water. It will take 5 to 6 weeks to work.

The wine is good, mixed half and half with grape juice.

GRAPE JUICE

Pick grapes off stems, wash and add 1 cup water to every 3 quarts of grapes. Boil until soft, strain and add 1 cup sugar to every 2 quarts juice. Let come to a boil, skim, and seal in sterilized bottles.

Sweets

MOLASSES AND CHOCOLATE TAFFY

1 cup molasses	1 tablespoon vinegar
½ cup sugar	1 teaspoon vanilla
3 squares unsweetened chocolate	¼ cup butter

Boil all together till a drop in cold water forms a hard ball. Pour out in a buttered pan to cool.

FLAGROOT CANDY

Dig roots at the end of the growing season when they will shrink least; wash thoroughly and scrape. Slice thin, or cut in match-stick pieces. Boil in water for an hour, change water and boil another hour. Drain and cook until transparent in a syrup made with 8 cups sugar and ½ cup water. Lay on waxed paper to dry. Store in tin or glass between layers of waxed paper.

Lovage root may be candied in the same manner.

From Plymouth Herb Gardens
OLD SAYINGS ABOUT HERBS

"Why should a man die while sage grows in the garden?"

Old Chinese Proverb

"Eat sage in May, and live for aye."

Old English saying

"To comfort the brain smell camomile, eat sage, wash measurably, sleep reasonably, delight to hear melody and singing."

William Ram (1608)

Sweet Herbs in New England Gardens

In NEW ENGLAND'S RARITIES DISCOVERED, published in 1672, John Josselyn gives the following list of herbs which he found growing in New England gardens: sorrel, parsley, marygold, chervil, burnet, winter and summer savory, thyme, sage, spearmint, rue, fetherfew, southernwood, rosemary, lavender, pennyroyal, fennel, coriander, dill, annis, clary, and tansy.

"Rue," he says, "will hardly grow." Fetherfew "prospereth exceedingly." Southernwood "is no plant for this country, nor rosemary, nor bayes." Lavender "is not for this climate." Fennel "must be taken up and kept in a warm cellar all winter." Annis "thrives exceedingly, but annis seed and also the seed of fennel seldom come to maturity. The seed of annis is commonly eaten by a fly." Clary "never lasts but one summer."

Mr. Josselyn is not to be taken literally, for many of the herbs he says will not prosper, do so in New England.

HOW TO USE HERBS

Herbs, like all seasonings, should be used with discretion, never on the principle that if a little is good, more is better. A good rule is to use ¼ teaspoon of the dried herbs or 1 teaspoon of the fresh for a serving for 4, and gradually increase the amount if you think you would like more.

Herbs may be used green in salads; the tender tips of basil, thyme, tarragon, sage, marjoram, salad burnet, chervil, fennel, lovage, cress (pepper grass), as well as parsley and chives. For potato or cabbage salad, use fennel, dill, or celery seed. The green herbs may also be minced to use in omelets. A combination of parsley, tarragon and marjoram or thyme; savory, parsley, and a tiny bit of hyssop; or sage and parsley in a cheese omelet are good.

HERB MUSTARD

4 ounces mustard	2 tablespoons sugar
2 tablespoons flour	herb vinegar
2 teaspoons salt	2 teaspoons minced herbs

Blend the dry ingredients thoroughly, then add herb vinegar to make a smooth paste. Then add 2 teaspoons minced green herbs and, if liked, horseradish and garlic to taste.

Herb mustard may be used as a condiment, or to spread over any meat or fish for broiling, or over a roast. Spread herb mustard and finely minced fennel or tarragon on mackerel, salmon, swordfish, or halibut before broiling.

HERB VINEGAR

Basil, fennel, dill, tarragon, hot peppers, and garlic may all be used for vinegars.

Fill a quart jar with the fresh herb and pour a good cider vinegar over it. Let it stand until the vinegar is strong enough for your taste, two weeks or more.

For garlic vinegar, add 6 or 8 cloves of garlic, peeled and split, 8 or 10 whole cloves, and the same of peppercorns, to a quart of vinegar and let stand.

To get clear herb vinegar, strain through filter paper.

BOUQUETS GARNI

1) 1 sprig parsley
   1 sprig summer savory
   1 sprig chervil
   1 sprig basil
   1 stalk celery with leaves
   6 chive leaves

2) 1 sprig summer savory
   1 sprig thyme
   1 sprig parsley
   1 sprig marjoram

3) 1 sprig chervil
   2 sprigs marjoram
   6 chive leaves

Use in soups, stews, or sauces. Remove before serving.

SMOKED SHOULDER WITH HERB VINEGAR

Stick a dozen or more whole cloves into shoulder and pin two bay leaves to it with cloves. Pour over 3 teaspoons herb vinegar and 3 tablespoons sherry. Let stand an hour or more, basting occasionally with the liquid. Place in kettle with any vinegar and sherry remaining. Cover with boiling water and simmer until tender.

HAMBURG STEAK WITH HERB MUSTARD

Shape a pound of hamburg steak into flat cakes about 1½ inches thick. Spread with Herb Mustard, sprinkle with a little thyme, fresh or dried, and broil. Turn, spread with mustard and thyme and broil.

MOCK PATE DE FOIS GRAS

Stand 1 pound of beef liver in boiling water for 8 minutes. Drain, and put liver and 1 onion through food chopper. Add:

6 tablespoons melted bacon fat   4 tablespoons minced parsley
1 teaspoon thyme   1 teaspoon salt
           ½ teaspoon pepper

Cook in a double boiler for 30 minutes, cool and use as a spread for toast or crackers.

COURT BOUILLON FOR
SALMON, HALIBUT, OR SHRIMP

1 large bay leaf   ¼ cup sherry
2 or 3 whole cloves   ¼ teaspoon each dried tarragon,
2 or 3 whole peppercorns   thyme, and parsley
1 teaspoon herb vinegar

Mix all ingredients and add to boiling water, enough to cover fish. Simmer fish in liquid until tender. The remaining liquid may be strained and thickened for sauce.

COTTAGE CHEESE WITH HERBS

½ pound cottage cheese   ¼ teaspoon salt
12 leaves of chive   ⅛ teaspoon garlic powder
1 sprig each of salad burnet,   2 teaspoons Worcestershire
   thyme, marjoram, basil,   sauce
   savory, and sage, all finely
   minced

Mix all together thoroughly with a fork. Use for hors d'oeuvres, sandwiches, in salads, and salad dressings, or to stuff celery. It may be varied by adding blue cheese to taste.

To cooked carrots, add butter and minced fresh parsley, or cook with a sprig of mint.

To summer squash, add minced fresh marjoram, or cook the marjoram with the squash.

To fresh peas, add a sprig of mint while cooking.

To snap, shell, or Lima beans, add 2 good sprigs of savory while cooking.

Some Cook Books of the Seventeenth Century—Found in New England

These small volumes, brought from England, must have been long preserved and carefully studied by New England cooks, and passed on to their descendants "with certain Useful Traditions."

THE QUEEN'S CLOSET OPENED   London 1671
Incomparable Secrets in Physick, Chirurgery, Preserving, and Candying, etc., which are presented unto the Queen By the most Experienced Persons of the Times, many of whom were held in esteem, when She pleased to descend to private Recreations.

THE COMPLEAT COOK   London 1671
Exactly Prescribing the Most Ready Wayes whether Italian, Spanish, French, For dressing of Flesh or Fish, ordering of Sauces or making of Pastry

THE WHOLE BODY OF COOKERY DISSECTED   London 1673
. . . Wherein is contained certain Bills of Fare for the seasons of the year for Feasts and common Diets . . .

THE ACCOMPLISHED COOK   London 1685
Or the Art and Mystery of Cookery

THE COMPLETE COOK'S GUIDE   London 1683

THE ENGLISH HUSWIFE, by Gervase Markham,   London 1615

THE HOUSEWIFE, by Letitia Montagne   London 1781

THE COOK'S AND CONFECTIONER'S DICTIONARY,
     by John Nott   London 1733

Contentment

When day was gone,
And from their occupations out of doors
The Son and Father were come home, even then,
Their labor did not cease; unless when all
Turned to the cleanly supper-board, and there
Each with a mess of pottage and skimmed milk,
Sat round the basket filled with oaten cakes
And their plain home-made cheese. Yet when the meal
Was ended, both betook themselves
To such convenient work as might employ
Their hands by the fire-side, perhaps to card
Wool for the housewife's spindle, or repair
Some injury done to sickle, flail, or scythe,
Or other implement of house and field.
Neither gay, perhaps
Nor cheerful, yet with objects and with hope,
Living a life of eager industry.

MICHAEL: *A Pastoral Poem,*
William Wordsworth, 1800

INDEX